Zaner-Bloser Handwriting

1

Zaner-Bloser, Inc., P.O. Box 16764, Columbus, Ohio 43216-6764

1-800-421-3018

Copyright © 2003 Zaner-Bloser, Inc.   ISBN 0-7367-1218-6

Printed in the United States of America

05 06 (106) 5

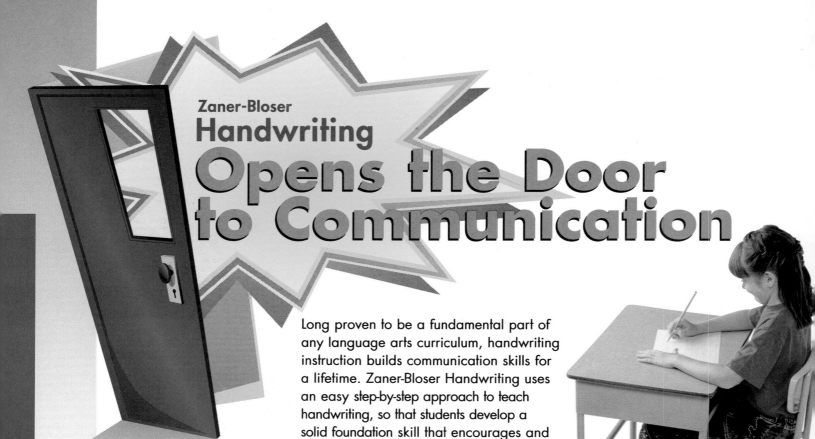

Zaner-Bloser
Handwriting
Opens the Door to Communication

Long proven to be a fundamental part of any language arts curriculum, handwriting instruction builds communication skills for a lifetime. Zaner-Bloser Handwriting uses an easy step-by-step approach to teach handwriting, so that students develop a solid foundation skill that encourages and supports all of their writing, reading, and assessment efforts.

With Zaner-Bloser Handwriting, students are prepared for a lifetime of communication success!

Handwriting Success:

The four Keys to Legibility—shape, size, spacing, and slant—are presented within an easy, step-by-step process for teaching and learning good handwriting.

Writing Success:

Zaner-Bloser's systematic program builds automaticity in reproduction of the alphabet, so students are free to focus on meaning and expression as they write.

Reading Success:

Zaner-Bloser's vertical manuscript alphabet improves letter recognition and supports reading development because it is the same alphabet children see outside the classroom, every day.

Better Assessment:

The Keys to Legibility help students self-assess and improve their own handwriting. Then they apply their good handwriting skills in all testing situations, including standardized tests.

Aa Bb Cc Dd Ee Ff Gg

"Handwriting is a basic communication skill that is used early in the school life of a student. To facilitate communication, it is imperative that students write legibly with ease and fluency."

Research-based Findings on Handwriting, Harford County Public Schools, Bel Air, MD

"The mental processes involved in handwriting, experts point out, are connected to other important learning functions, such as storing information in memory, retrieving information, manipulating letters, and linking them to sound when spelling."

Handwriting Instruction: Key to Good Writing, Cheryl Murfin Bond

"Solid familiarity with the visual shapes of the individual letters is an absolute prerequisite for learning to read."

Beginning to Read: Thinking and Learning About Print, Marilyn Jager Adams

Research confirms that good handwriting opens the door to communication.

"Beginning writers need regular and guided handwriting practice."

Handwriting: A Communication Tool, Saskatchewan Education

"Good handwriting and the ability to write strong compositions, it turns out, go hand-in-hand."

Handwriting Instruction: Key to Good Writing, Cheryl Murfin Bond

Aa Bb Cc Dd Ee Ff Gg

Opens the Door to Handwriting Success

Keys to Legibility
Make your writing easy to read. Look at the shape of each letter.

Shape

I can write letters.

These letters have good shape.

This writing is easy to read.

Vertical Lines
Some letters have | lines.
I F i

Horizontal Lines
Some letters have — lines.
E t H

Circle Lines
Some letters have ○ lines.
O c s

Slant Lines
Some letters have ╱ lines.
W x V

30

Shape
Size
Spacing
Slant

4

Keys to Legibility

Grade I
Student Edition
page shown.

Shape, Size, Spacing, and Slant are the basis of Zaner-Bloser's unique instructional system.

- **The Keys form an assessment rubric for teachers and students.**

- **Each section of the Student Edition features one of the Keys. Students learn how to use the Key to look at and evaluate their work.**

- **Keys are placed on student pages in each lesson to reinforce instruction and focus evaluation.**

- **Keys are used in the Teacher Edition as prompts for the teacher to remind students about shape, size, spacing, and slant.**

- **Teachers have clear guidelines based on the four Keys to Legibility for evaluating students' handwriting.**

The Program Components Students and Teachers Need for Handwriting Success

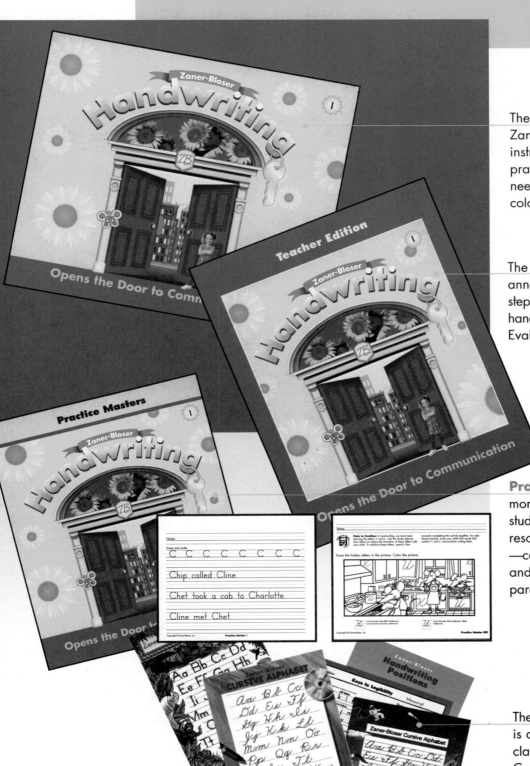

The **Student Edition** features Zaner-Bloser's easy, step-by-step instruction, as well as the meaningful practice and application students need for handwriting success, all in a colorful, fun book that students love.

The **Teacher Edition** is fully annotated and provides teachers a step-by-step guide that makes teaching handwriting simply successful. A handy Evaluation Guide is also included.

Practice Masters provide even more practice for every letter and skill students learn, as well as additional resources to make teaching successful —certificates, an evaluation record, and school to home letters to keep parents and guardians involved.

The **Poster/Wall Chart Super Pack** is a perfect addition to the handwriting classroom, with Manuscript and Cursive Alphabet Posters, a Keys to Legibility Poster, and a Handwriting Positions Poster.

Handwriting Ancillary Materials That Support the Instructional Plan

All of these Handwriting ancillary materials are provided FREE upon request with purchase of 25 matching Student Editions—the essentials you need to reinforce Zaner-Bloser's handwriting instruction are included!

Teacher Edition with Grade Level Evaluation Guide included

Practice Masters

Poster/Wall Chart Super Pack

Handwriting Ancillary Materials to Further Enhance the Handwriting Classroom

These ancillaries are referenced at the beginning of every unit in the Teacher Edition:

- **A** Alphabet Wall Strips, K–6
- **B** Illustrated Alphabet Strips, K–4
- **C** Desk Strips, 1–6
- **D** Wipe-Off Practice Cards—Manuscript and Cursive, K–6
- **E** Zaner-Bloser Fontware, K–6
- **F** Manuscript/Cursive Card Sets, 1–4
- **G** Home Handwriting Pack, K–4

- **H** Handwriting Tools, K–6
- **I** Journals and Blank Books, K–6
- **J** Paper, K–6
- **K** Modality Kit
- **L** Listening Alphabeat, 1–4
- **M** Post Office Kit, K–4
- **N** Escritura—Spanish Blackline Masters, 1–6
- **O** Fun With Handwriting
- **P** Touch & Trace Letter Cards, PreK–3

- **Q** Now I Know My ABC's, PreK–1
- **R** Now I Know My 123's, PreK–1
- **S** Read, Write, and Color Alphabet Mat, K–2
- **T** Letter Cards, K–2
- **U** Book of Transparencies, 1–6
- **V** Handwriting Research and Resources
- **W** Opens the Door to Teaching Handwriting— CD-ROM for Classroom or Teacher Inservice Use

Only Zaner-Bloser provides you with this much support for teaching handwriting!

Fine Motor Development Kit

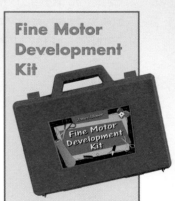

Zaner-Bloser's Fine Motor Development Kit can help your students develop the fine motor skills essential for writing and many other school activities.

The Student Edition
Opens the Door
to Handwriting Success
for Students

Zaner-Bloser Handwriting guides students through an easy step-by-step process for learning good, legible handwriting that will last a lifetime.

Letter models with arrows show stroke description and sequence.

Shaded letters for tracing are provided.

Starting dots tell students where to begin the letter.

Stop and Check signs remind students to evaluate their letters.

School to Home stroke descriptions help parents reinforce and evaluate students' handwriting at home.

A Practice page in each section gives students another chance to practice and review the letters they just learned.

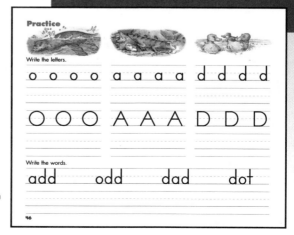

Grade I
Student Edition
pages shown.

Writing practice is done directly beneath a model that gives students a visual guide that both left- and right-handed students can easily see.

Sentences provide students with even more writing practice.

We like to write!

Write the words.

ant   animal   ask

Write the sentence.

All my friends play ball.

On Your Own Write words to finish the sentence.

I can play

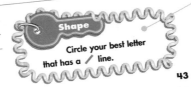

Shape

Circle your best letter that has a / line.

43

Personal writing activities help make language arts connections.

A Key to Legibility prompts students to evaluate their own handwriting.

An Application page at the end of every section provides writing practice that makes important connections to language arts and the other content areas. Students also write their own words, and a Key to Legibility prompts them to evaluate their handwriting.

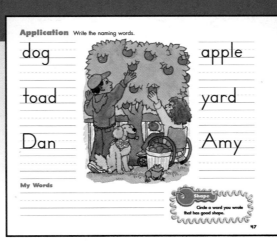

Application Write the naming words.

dog   apple

toad   yard

Dan   Amy

My Words

Shape

Circle a word you wrote that has good shape.

47

Grade 1
Student Edition
pages shown.

The Teacher Edition
Opens the Door to Handwriting Success
for Teachers

Section Openers provide the information, guidance, and extra tips teachers need.

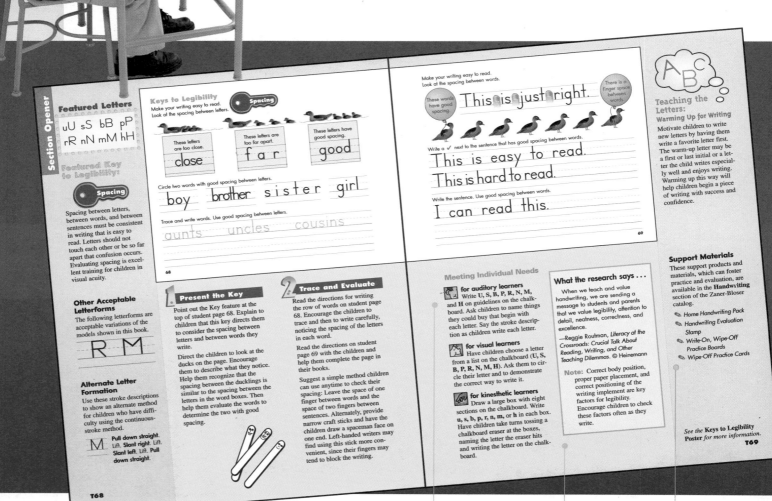

Grade 1
Teacher Edition
pages shown.

Multimodal activities are provided for meeting individual needs.

Research connects handwriting instruction to other forms of communication.

Additional materials are listed that support the instructional plan.

Opens the Door to Successful Time Management
for Teachers

Three-step lesson takes about 15 minutes!

The three steps of the lesson present clear, simple teaching guidelines.

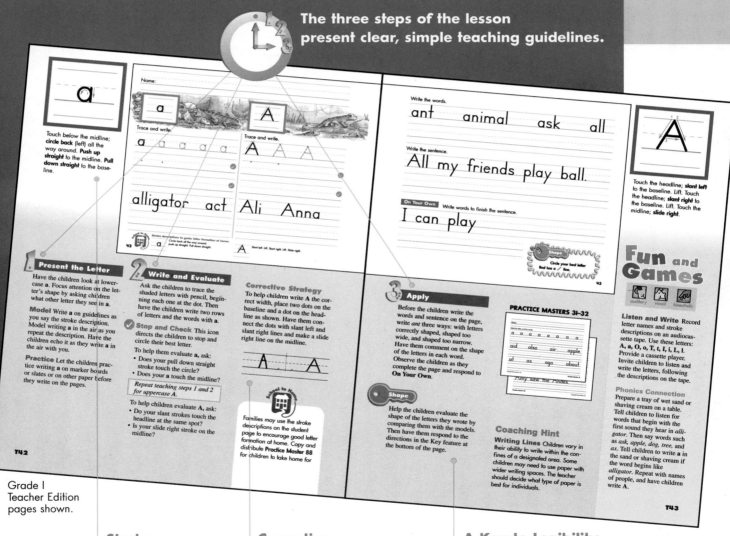

Grade 1
Teacher Edition
pages shown.

Stroke descriptions are short and clearly marked.

Corrective strategies & coaching hints provide the means to correct common problems.

A Key to Legibility helps teachers guide their students through the evaluation process.

Zaner-Bloser Handwriting Opens the Door to Writing and Reading Success

Teaching Handwriting in the 21st Century— An Occupational Therapist's Perspective

By Maureen King, O.T.R.

Children come to school with a broad range of developmental skill levels. Many children are already using many fine motor skills, gross motor skills, and perceptual skills, developed through exposure to a variety of play experiences. Some children, however, have not properly developed these fundamental skills that directly impact how well they learn in school.

Hand (motor) skills, as they develop, build upon each other, beginning at birth when babies grasp reflexively. As children grow and interact with their surroundings, they move on to using their thumbs and index fingers, and then their hands in a variety of positions. The development of perceptual skills, a child's ability to perceive how things fit together, is best facilitated by assembling and moving objects around.

In the past, there were more "play-filled" opportunities to prompt development of these skills. Today, however, children's play is becoming more automated. Many board games are now played on computer screens, shoes are fastened with Velcro, and crayons are put aside in order to pursue interactive activities. This decreased use of manipulatives at home and at school can diminish a child's opportunity to practice grasp and release and controlled placement—skills that are necessary for efficient pencil use.

Symptoms of these trends can manifest themselves in a young child's first hand-writing experiences at school. Handwriting requires eye-hand coordination, fine motor skills, and the perceptual ability to simultaneously understand and produce letterforms. When children who have not developed key foundational skills first attempt to write manuscript letters, frustration can result. Often, their efforts consist of incomplete or careless methods of forming letters, which can lead to bad habits. Something must be done for these children so that they can achieve handwriting success.

I am pleased to offer structured corrective strategies that will help teachers strengthen skills that lead to improved handwriting. You will find these strategies, or **Special Helps,** throughout the **Zaner-Bloser Handwriting** Teacher Edition. They suggest ways to isolate component skills, reinforce the instructional material, and highlight special points and concerns. In using these ideas in your classroom, include a mix of learning styles so that children can see it, hear it, feel it, do it in their palms and on the chalkboard, with their eyes open and closed. These activities will help bring handwriting success to all children, including those who rarely play board games, color with crayons, or tie their shoes.

Maureen King is referenced throughout the K–3 Teacher Editions.

The Critical Role of Handwriting in Student Success

By Steve Graham, Professor and Distinguished Scholar/Teacher, University of Maryland

Handwriting plays a critical role in writing development. One way of illustrating its impact on writing is to imagine that you have been asked to write something using a Chinese typewriter. This is the most complicated typewriter in the world, containing 5,850 characters. As you search for characters, some of the ideas and writing plans you are trying to hold in memory will undoubtedly be lost, as most of your attention is consumed by trying to transcribe words into print. It will also be difficult to create additional plans or sharpen the text you are currently producing, as most of your attention is directed at locating the next character to be typed.

Although most of us will never use a Chinese typewriter, we have at one time or another experienced frustration at being unable to write our thoughts down fast enough due to our limited handwriting ability. For children, handwriting can be so "taxing" that it influences the pace and course of their writing development. The physical act of handwriting is so strenuous for many beginning writers that they develop an approach to writing that minimizes the use of other composing processes, such as planning, because these processes are also mentally demanding. Just as importantly, children who experience difficulty mastering handwriting often avoid writing and develop a mind-set that they cannot write, leading to arrested writing development.

Poor handwriting is also the thief of one of our most valuable commodities—time. Teachers lose precious time trying to decipher papers that are illegible. The handwriting of some children is so slow that it takes them almost twice as long to produce the same text as their more facile classmates, exerting a heavy toll on their productivity.

Despite the importance of handwriting to school success, writing development, and written communication, the teaching of handwriting has been de-emphasized in some schools. Although handwriting continues to be taught in most classrooms nationwide, it is taught sporadically, if at all, in others. In these classrooms, it is often assumed that handwriting will develop naturally, by immersing children in a literacy-rich environment where they have plenty of opportunities to write and read for real purposes. While this assumption has a comforting simplicity, absolving schools from the responsibility of directly teaching handwriting, there is no scientific evidence to support it. In contrast, there is almost a century of research that demonstrates the power of directly and systematically teaching handwriting.

For years, I have heard rumors about the demise of handwriting, as it would soon be replaced by word processing or speech synthesis (prior to that it was the typewriter). While these tools have clearly become a more prominent part of everyday life, handwriting has not been superseded. Much writing is still done by hand, especially in schools, and this is unlikely to change anytime in the near future.

Steve Graham is referenced in the Teacher Editions.

Manuscript and Cursive Alphabets
Promote Writing and Reading Development

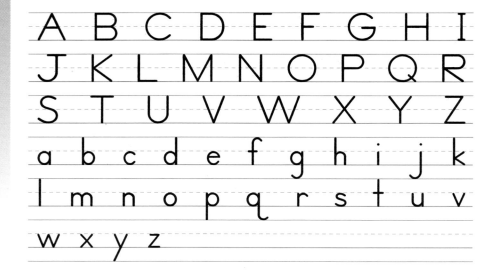

ABCDEFGHI
JKLMNOPQR
STUVWXYZ
abcdefghijk
lmnopqrstuv
wxyz

Zaner-Bloser's continuous-stroke, vertical manuscript alphabet . . .

- Promotes automaticity in students' writing because students only have to learn four simple strokes

- Reinforces students' reading because it is the alphabet students see every day inside and outside the classroom

Two Simplified Alphabets for Handwriting and Communication Success

*ABCDEFGHI
JKLMNOPQ
RSTUVWXYZ
abcdefghi
jklmnopqr
stuvwxyz*

Zaner-Bloser's simplified cursive alphabet . . .

- Reinforces writing and reading development because it is easier to write and read

- Helps students get higher test scores because, as legible cursive writing becomes automatic, students can focus more energy on their message

Zaner-Bloser Handwriting
Opens the Door to Better Assessment

Writing Quickly
Make your writing easy to read.
Write this rhyme.

Rain, rain, go away.
Come again another day.

Now write it again.
faster.

Write the rhyme one more time.
Try to write faster.
Make sure your writing is easy to read.

Now read your writing. Ask others to read it, too.
Then circle Yes or No next to each sentence.

My writing is easy for me to read.   Yes   No

My writing is easy for others to read.   Yes   No

115

Grade I
Student Edition
pages shown.

Better Self-Assessment:

- The Keys to Legibility provide students with a system for learning and assessing their handwriting.

- Stop and Check signs throughout the lessons are reminders for students to continuously self-evaluate as they work.

More Success on Standardized Tests:

Writing Quickly, in the Student Edition, provides a challenging exercise to help students develop automaticity in writing and do well in high pressure testing situations where they must maintain legibility and also write quickly.

Shape
Size
Spacing
Slant

Opens the Door to Handwriting Success for Every Student

Handwriting success is achieved most often when the initial instruction involves a multimodal approach. Students need to develop a correct mental and motor image of the stroke, joining, letter, or word before they attempt to write.

Throughout the Teacher Edition, Zaner-Bloser Handwriting provides techniques that will help address the multimodal needs of different students.

For the Kinesthetic Learner—Remember that instruction for the student whose primary sensory modality is kinesthetic should be tactile, involving movement and the sense of touch.

- Walk out the letter strokes on the floor.
- Form letters in the air using full-arm movement.
- Make letter models with clay or string.
- Write strokes, letters, and joinings in sand.
- Use different writing instruments, such as crayons, markers, and varied sizes of pencils.
- Trace large strokes, letters, and joinings on the chalkboard and on paper—first with fingers, then with chalk or other media.
- Dip fingers in water and form letters and joinings on the chalkboard.

For the Auditory Learner—Students whose primary sensory modality is auditory require instruction that enables them to listen and to verbalize.

- Verbalize each stroke in the letter as that letter is presented.
- Encourage the student to verbalize the letter strokes and to explain how strokes are alike and how they are different in the letterforms.
- Ask students to write random letters as you verbalize the strokes.
- Be consistent in the language you use to describe letters, strokes, shapes, and joinings.

For the Visual Learner—As a general rule, a student whose primary sensory modality is visual will have little difficulty in handwriting if instruction includes adequate visual stimuli.

- Encourage students first to look at the letter as a whole and to ask themselves if the letter is tall or short, fat or skinny. Does all of the letter rest on the baseline, is it a tall letter, or is it a letter with a descender? How many and what kinds of strokes are in the letter?
- Have students look at each individual stroke carefully before they attempt to write the letter.

The Left-Handed Student

Three important techniques assist the left-handed student in writing.

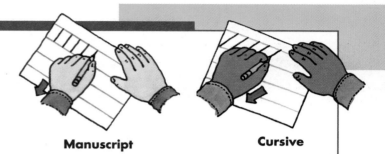

Paper Position:

For manuscript writing, the lower right corner of the paper should point toward the left of the body's midsection.

For cursive writing, the lower right corner of the paper should point toward the body's midsection.

Downstrokes are pulled toward the left elbow.

Manuscript   **Cursive**

Pencil Position:

The top of the pencil should point toward the left elbow. The pen or pencil should be held at least one inch above the point. This allows students to see what they are writing.

Arm Position:

Holding the left arm close to the body and keeping the hand below the line of writing prevents "hooking" the wrist and smearing the writing.

General Coaching Tips for Teachers

- Teach a handwriting lesson daily, if possible, for approximately 15 minutes. Spend a minimum of 5 minutes of this time in actual instruction before the students practice.

- Surround children with models of good handwriting. Set an example when you write on the chalkboard and on students' papers.

- Teach the letters through basic strokes.

- Emphasize one **Key to Legibility** at a time.

- Use appropriately ruled paper. Increase the size of the grids for any student who is experiencing difficulty.

- Continuous self-evaluation is necessary for optimal progress.

- Stress comfortable writing posture and pencil position. Increase the size of the pencil for students who "squeeze" the writing implement.

- Show the alternate method of holding the pencil, and allow students to choose the one that is better for them. (Refer to the alternate method shown in the Teacher Edition.)

- Provide opportunities for children in the upper grades to use manuscript writing. Permit manuscript for some assignments if children prefer manuscript to cursive.

- Encourage students with poor sustained motor control to use conventional manuscript, with frequent lifts, if continuous manuscript is difficult for them.

Meeting Individual Needs

Students With Reversal Tendencies

Directionality—A problem with directionality (moving from left to right across the page) interferes with a child's ability to form letters correctly and to write text that makes sense. To develop correct directionality, try these techniques:

- Provide opportunities for the child to write at the chalkboard within a confined area with frequent arrows as a reminder of left-to-right progression.

- Prepare sheets of paper on which the left edges and the beginning stroke of a letter, such as **b**, are colored green.

Letter Reversals—Determine which letters a student most often reverses. Make a list of these reversals and concentrate on them either on an individual basis or by grouping together the students who are reversing the same letters.

- Emphasize each step of the stroke description before the children write a letter.

- Provide a letter for tracing that has been colored according to stroke order. Repeat the stroke description with the children as they write the letter.

- Encourage the children to write the letter as they verbalize the stroke description.

Students With Attention Deficit Problems

Because they have difficulty focusing and maintaining attention, these students must concentrate on individual strokes in the letterforms. When they have learned the strokes, they can put them together to form letters, and then learn the joinings (in cursive) to write words. The activities recommended for kinesthetic learners (on page Z16) are appropriate for students with an attention deficit problem. Following are additional suggestions:

- Give very short assignments.

- Supervise closely and give frequent encouragement.

Zaner-Bloser

Handwriting

1

Author

Clinton S. Hackney, Ed.D.

Reviewers

Julie Althide, Teacher, Hazelwood School District, St. Louis, Missouri

Becky Brashears, Teacher, Gocio Elementary, Sarasota, Florida

Douglas Dewey, Teacher, National Heritage Academies, Grand Rapids, Michigan

Jennifer B. Dutcher, Teacher, Elk Grove School District, Sacramento, California

Gita Farbman, Teacher, School District of Philadelphia, Philadelphia, Pennsylvania

Susan Ford, Teacher, St. Ann's School, Charlotte, North Carolina

Brenda Forehand, Teacher, David Lipscomb Middle School, Nashville, Tennessee

Sharon Hall, Teacher, USD 443, Dodge City, Kansas

Sr. James Madeline, Teacher, St. Anthony School, Allston, Massachusetts

Lori A. Martin, Teacher, Chicago Public Schools, Chicago, Illinois

Vikki F. McCurdy, Teacher, Mustang School District, Oklahoma City, Oklahoma

Melissa Neary Morgan, Reading Specialist, Fairfax County Public Schools, Fairfax, Virginia

Sue Postlewait, Literacy Resource Consultant, Marshall County Schools, Moundsville, West Virginia

Gloria C. Rivera, Principal, Edinburg CISO, Edinburg, Texas

Rebecca Rollefson, Teacher, Ericsson Community School, Minneapolis, Minnesota

Susan Samsa, Teacher, Dover City Schools, Dover, Ohio

Zelda J. Smith, Instructional Specialist, New Orleans Public Schools, New Orleans, Louisiana

Occupational Therapy Consultant: Maureen E. King, O.T.R.

Credits

Art: Diane Blasius: 4, 60, 62, 64, 66, 67, 100, 102, 104, 106, 107; Ruth Flanigan: 6, 7; John Hovell: 30, 31, 50, 51, 68, 69, 90, 91, 118; Tom Leonard: 3, 32, 34, 36, 38, 39, 70, 72, 76, 78; Sharron O'Neil: 4, 22, 23, 24, 25, 26, 27, 28, 29, 112, 113; Diane Paterson: 47; Nicole Rutten: 40, 42, 44, 46; Andy San Diego: 3, 8, 9, 14, 16, 18, 19, 20, 74, 78, 80, 82, 84, 86, 88, 89, 110, 111, 114, 115; John Wallner: 48, 52, 54, 56, 58, 59, 92, 94, 96, 98, 99

Photos: George C. Anderson Photography, Inc.: 5, 10, 11, 12, 13

Development: Kirchoff/Wohlberg, Inc., in collaboration with Zaner-Bloser Educational Publishers

ISBN 0-7367-1210-0

Contents

Writing Letters and Words

Legibility Is Important

The goal of *Zaner-Bloser Handwriting* is to teach children to write legibly. As you work through the pages of this book with the children, you will be helping them learn to write letters, words, and sentences that are legible to both writers and readers. By learning and applying the four Keys to Legibility—**shape, size, spacing, and slant**—the children will evaluate their writing and discover techniques to help them improve and refine their writing skills.

The **Getting Started** pages are important for laying a foundation for writing. **Show What You Can Do** provides an initial sample of the child's handwriting quality before formal handwriting instruction. **Letters and Numerals** presents correct models of the forms the children will write. **Manuscript Positions** guides beginning writers in the correct positions for sitting, holding the writing implement, and positioning the paper. **Your Book** defines and explains the visual components on the children's pages that help beginning writers learn to write with consistent legibility and to evaluate and improve their writing throughout the year. Children are introduced to the basic strokes used to form manuscript letters.

In **Writing Numerals,** children observe models and begin to write the numerals **1** through **10** with correct strokes.

Lowercase and uppercase letters are introduced together in **Writing Letters and Words**. The letter sequence is determined by common elements of the lowercase letters.

Finally, children apply their knowledge in **Using What You've Learned,** which includes **Number Words, Days of the Week, Months, Writing Quickly,** and a final **Show What You Can Do**.

Note that models are provided for all writing, and children have space to write directly beneath the models. **On Your Own** encourages children to write about their own experiences.

It is suggested that children keep a writing notebook or folder of the writing they do for themselves and for others.

Use this introductory page with your class as an invitation to the *Zaner-Bloser Handwriting* program.

Explain to children that in this book they will learn how to write letters, words, and sentences. They will also discover ways to help make their writing easy to read.

Practice Masters

- Getting Started, 1–17
- Numerals, 18–22
- Letters, 23–74
- Numeral Practice, 75
- Student Record, 76
- Certificates, 77–78
- Zaner-Bloser Alphabet, 79
- Stroke Descriptions, 80–83
- School-to-Home Practice Pages, 84–109
- Blank Writing Grid, 110

These support products are available in Zaner-Bloser's K–8 Catalog.

- Poster/Wall Chart Super Pack
- *Now I Know My ABCs*
- *Now I Know My 1, 2, 3's*
- Touch and Trace Letter Cards
- Alphabet Wall Strip
- Letter Cards
- Read, Write, and Color Alphabet Mat
- Zaner-Bloser Fontware
- Home Handwriting Pack
- Journals and Blank Books
- Paper
- Modality Kit
- *Opens the Door to Teaching Handwriting (CD-ROM)*
- *Handwriting Research and Resources*
- *Fun With Handwriting*
- Handwriting Transparencies
- *Escritura*

Write "The Alphabet Song" on the chalkboard or on large chart paper. As you point to the letters, invite children to sing this familiar song with you.

A–B–C–D–E–F–G
H–I–J–K
L–M–N–O–P
Q–R–S
T–U–V
W–X–Y and Z.
Now I know my ABC's.
Next time won't you sing with me?

Books to Share

Zaner-Bloser's **Ray's Readers** from A to Z

Zaner-Bloser's **My Alphabet** books

Chouinard, Roger and Mariko Chouinard. *The Amazing Animal Alphabet Book*. Doubleday & Company, Inc., 1988.

Cleary, Beverly. *The Hullabaloo ABC*. Morrow Junior books, 1998.

Grover, Max. *The Accidental Zucchini: An Unexpected Alphabet*. Harcourt Brace & Company, 1993.

Hoban, Tana. *I Read Signs*. Morrow/Avon, 1987.

Marzollo, Jean. *Ten Cats Have Hats: A Counting Book*. Scholastic Inc., 1994.

Rotner, Shelley. *Action Alphabet*. Atheneum Books for Young Readers, 1996.

Walton, Rick. *So Many Bunnies: A Bedtime ABC and Counting Book*. Lothrop, Lee & Shepard Books, 1998.

Yolen, Jane. *Elfabet: An ABC of Elves*. Little, Brown & Company, 1990.

T6

Pretest

Show What You Can Do

Write your name here.

Write letters you know here.

Write how old you are here.

6

Pretest

Show What You Can Do

Tell the children that during handwriting time, they will be learning to write the letters of the alphabet and the numerals.

Preview the book with the children. Explain that the first thing they will do, on student page 6, is show what they can write.

Help children locate the writing spaces for their name, for letters they know, and for their age.

Discuss with children ideas for writing and for what they might draw on page 7.

Evaluate

Observe how children write their name and age. Note that many children may still be writing their name in all uppercase letters.

Children may have been taught to write some or all of the alphabet letters and numerals in kindergarten. You may use these pages as a pretest to help you assess each child's current handwriting skills.

Zaner-Bloser's *Evaluation Guide* for grade 1 handwriting is a handy tool for evaluating students' writing. The evaluation criteria are the Keys to Legibility. Samples of children's handwriting, ranging in quality from excellent to poor, provide a helpful comparison for evaluation.

Show what else you can write here. Draw a picture about your writing.

Fun and Games

auditory visual kinesthetic

Coaching Hints

Hands-On Writing Use tagboard or self-adhesive ruled name strips to make a desktop nametag for each child in your class. Tape the nametags to the children's desks so they can use them as writing models. (visual)

Right Hand/Left Hand
Generally, children settle into a dominant hand by the age of about 6½ years, possibly later for left-handed children. To determine a child's preferred hand, observe the child carrying out a variety of activities, such as screwing and unscrewing a lid, bouncing a ball, winding a yo-yo, cutting paper, using a hand puppet, and holding a spoon. Established hand preference will be apparent as the child performs the tasks.

Special Helps

Fine-Motor Skills
Children who hold a writing tool or silverware in a palm/fist grasp may need more help refining hand skills. Encourage development of the arches by inviting children to use a plastic knife to slice play dough "snakes" into small segments. The index finger should be placed on the top of the blade of the knife to provide downward pressure during cutting.

To further refine hand skills, review the name of each finger as children move it in isolation. As a warm-up for writing, have children name each finger as they touch it to the thumb with their eyes open and then closed.

—*Maureen King, O.T.R.*

My Name Invite children to write their names with crayon on drawing paper. Suggest they use different colors for the letters. Have them paint over the paper with thin tempera paint. The crayoned letters will resist the paint, and the name will show through.

Alike and Different
Prepare two sets of cards, each with numerals from **1** through **10,** for a matching game. Show children how to play the game by turning all the cards facedown. Have the first player choose two cards. If the numerals match, have that child name the numeral, trace it, and keep the pair in his or her pile. Players take turns, and the player with the most pairs wins.

Before you sing, have the children open their books to the Letters and Numerals chart on pages 8 and 9. Ask them to look at the letters and join in singing "The Alphabet Song."

Next, try this letter identification game. Sing the following words to the tune of "Where Is Thumbkin?" Ask children to point to the letters named.

> Where is uppercase B?
> Where is lowercase b?
> Here they are!
> Here they are!
>
> Now find uppercase T.
> Now find lowercase t.
> Hip-hip-hooray!
> Hip-hip-hooray!

Invite children to look at the numerals on page 9 and to point to each numeral as you recite the following rhyme. Ask them to perform the traditional fist-over-fist hand motions as you say the rhyme again.

> One potato, two potato,
> Three potato, four,
> Five potato, six potato,
> Seven potato, more.
> Eight potato, nine potato,
> Ten potato, too.
> Counting all the numbers
> Is what I like to do.

Letters and Numerals

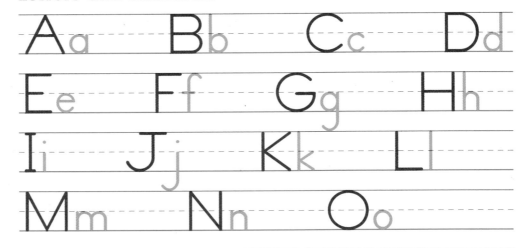

Trace the uppercase letter that begins your name.
Trace the lowercase letters in your name.

8

Trace, Write, Evaluate

Assist the children as needed in reading and following the directions on student pages 8 and 9. Then invite them to compare the letters they wrote with the models they traced in the alphabet.

To help children evaluate their writing, ask questions such as these:
- Did you begin your name with an uppercase letter?
- Are the other letters in your name lowercase?
- Do your letters look like the models?

Encourage children to talk about the letters they used and how the guidelines helped them.

Special Helps

Fine-Motor Skills
Children who fail to use their non-writing hand to steady the paper while writing or who switch hand preference while performing motor activities may have immature development of the complementary use of the hands.

To help, plan activities to stimulate the experience of two hands working together, which is important in handwriting. Ask the children to stack checkers, coins, or toy chips with their eyes closed. Point out how the nonpreferred hand provides valuable information about placement and stability.

—*Maureen King, O.T.R.*

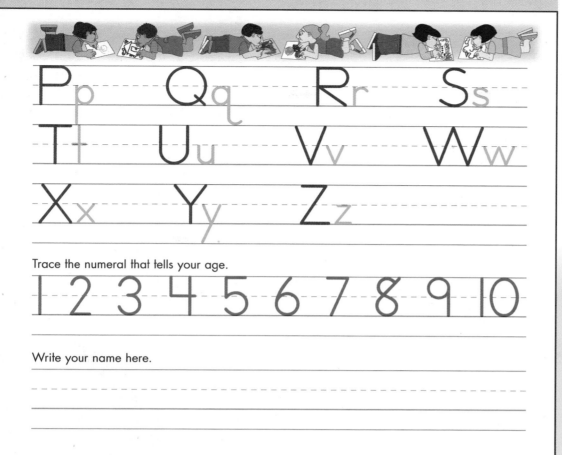

P p Q q R r S s

T t U u V v W w

X x Y y Z z

Trace the numeral that tells your age.

1 2 3 4 5 6 7 8 9 10

Write your name here.

9

Uppercase Letters

Circle the uppercase letter that begins your name.

A B C D E F G H I J
K L M N O P Q R S T
U V W X Y Z

Trace and circle the uppercase letter that begins each name.

Ross   Amy   Joe

Write your name.

Practice Master 3   Copyright © Zaner-Bloser, Inc.

Practice Master 4   Copyright © Zaner-Bloser, Inc.

Coaching Hint

Accessible Models Refer children to these pages often as a guide for writing. Children will find them especially helpful when they write independently.

The development of self-evaluation skills is an important goal of handwriting instruction. It helps children become independent learners. By having children compare their letters with models, you have already begun this process. Be patient. Some children will be more able than others to evaluate their writing. (visual)

Fun and Games

auditory   visual   kinesthetic

Tactile Letters Involve children in making a set of tactile alphabet letter cards for the writing center. Print each letter pair (lowercase and uppercase) on a blank index card and distribute the cards. Invite children to glue seeds, glitter, colored sand, or beans to the outline of each letter. When the letters are complete, have children take turns touching and naming letter pairs.

Alphabet Switch Have the children sit on chairs in a circle. Give each child a different lowercase letter card. Choose one child to stand in the center without a card. Call out the names of two letters and then say "Alphabet Switch." The children with the letters named will change places, while the child in the middle tries to get a seat. After each exchange, have children name the letters.

T9

Sing "The Alphabet Song" together to signal the beginning of handwriting time.

Then invite the children to stand in a circle and sing and play "Looby-Loo."

Here we dance Looby-loo,

Here we dance Looby-light.

Here we dance Looby-loo,

All on a Saturday night.

I put my right hand in,

I put my right hand out.

I give my right hand a
    shake, shake, shake,

And turn myself about.

Repeat, using the words **left hand, right foot, left foot, head,** and **whole self**.

See the **Handwriting Positions Wall Chart** *for more information.*

Writing Positions

If you write with your left hand...

Sit like this.
Sit comfortably. Lean forward a little. Keep your feet flat on the floor.

10

Place the paper like this.

Slant the paper as shown in the picture.

Rest both arms on the desk. Use your right hand to move the paper as you write.

Pull the pencil toward your left elbow when you write.

Hold the pencil like this.

Hold the pencil with your thumb and first two fingers.

Do not squeeze the pencil when you write.

Sitting Position

Using correct body position when writing will help children write better letters. They will also not tire as quickly. Encourage them to sit comfortably erect with their feet flat on the floor and their hips touching the back of the chair. Both arms should rest on the desk. Be sure children are relaxed, holding their pencils correctly.

Paper Position

Correct paper placement is a critical factor in legibility. To assure that the paper is placed correctly, for both right- and left-handed children, use tape to form a frame on the desk so the children will be able to place the paper in the correct position.

Pencil Position

Model good pencil position for the children. The writing implement is held between the thumb and the first two fingers, about an inch above its point. The first finger rests on top of the implement. The end of the bent thumb is placed against the writing instrument to hold it high in the hand and near the knuckle.

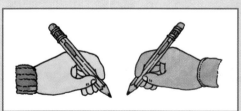

If you write with your right hand. . .

Sit like this.
Sit comfortably. Lean forward a little.
Keep your feet flat on the floor.

Place the paper like this.

Place the paper straight in front of you.

Rest both arms on the desk. Use your left hand to move the paper as you write.

Pull the pencil toward the middle of your body when you write.

Hold the pencil like this.

Hold the pencil with your thumb and first two fingers.

Do not squeeze the pencil when you write.

11

PRACTICE MASTERS 5–7

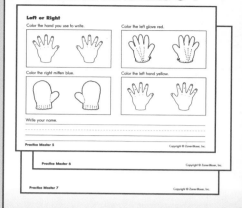

Fun and Games

auditory   visual   kinesthetic

Left Hand, Right Hand
Have children help each other trace the shape of their own left and right hands on construction paper. Then direct children to cut them out and paste them on another sheet of paper. Demonstrate how to write **L** on the left hand and **R** on the right hand. Ask children to draw a ring on one finger of the hand they use for writing.

Simon Says
To play this variation of "Simon Says," give children directions that include the words *left* and *right*. Have them stand facing you. Remind them to follow the direction only when they hear "Simon says." Here are some ideas to get you started.

Simon says, "Touch your nose with your right hand."
"Touch your chin with your left hand."
Simon says, "Take two steps to the left."

Coaching Hint

Left-Handed Writers Right-handed teachers will better understand left-handed children if they practice the left-handed position themselves. Group left-handers together for instruction if you can do so without calling attention to the practice. They should be seated to the left of the chalkboard.

Note: Children who have difficulty with the traditional pencil position may prefer the alternate method of holding the pencil between the first and second fingers. Once established, this grip can be easily transferred to the traditional tripod position.

Special Helps

Fine-Motor Skills
The development of fine motor skills is fundamentally important to handwriting success. Activities that encourage the development of the hands should be an important part of the early childhood classroom.

In handling writing tools and other objects, the ring and pinky fingers perform a stabilizing function, while the thumb and index finger are responsible for prehension or precision tasks. The third finger divides the hand. To develop and improve children's hand functions, provide opportunities to cut with scissors, draw with stencils, lace cards, use a pegboard, finger paint, and play with sand.

—*Maureen King, O.T.R.*

T11

Write **A**, **B**, and **C** on guidelines on the chalkboard.

Sing "The Alphabet Song," replacing the last lines with these:

> **I shall write my ABC's**
> **On the guidelines that I see.**

Explain to the children that using guidelines will help them write better letters.

Your Book
Models and Guidelines

There are writing models in your book. The models are on guidelines.

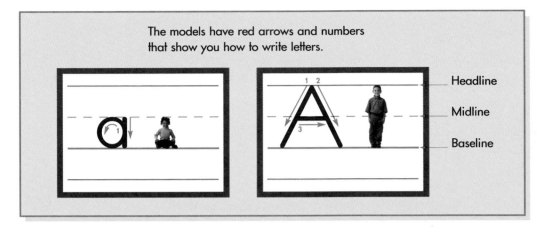

The models have red arrows and numbers that show you how to write letters.

Headline
Midline
Baseline

Start at the green dot when you trace and write.

12

Models and Guidelines

Direct children to look at the model letter boxes for **a** and **A** on student page 12. Point out the red arrows and numerals with the letters in the model boxes. Explain that they show how to write the letters, starting with the first numeral and following the arrows.

Guide children in locating and naming each guideline. Have them name its color and tell whether the line is solid or broken.

Draw guidelines on the chalkboard and ask volunteers to name each line in the grid. Remind children that every stroke and every letter begin somewhere on the writing grid in relation to one of these lines. By learning to write their letters correctly on the guidelines, they will learn to write letters that have consistent size. Consistent size helps make writing legible.

Have children notice the traffic light on student page 12. Ask them what the green light stands for. Point out the green dot in both **a** and **A**. Tell the children that when they begin to write letters, a green dot will help them remember where to begin writing.

Coaching Hint

Using Guidelines Distribute sheets of the lined writing paper children will be using in order to familiarize them with the guidelines. Help them locate the first set of guidelines. Demonstrate and have children follow along as you trace the headline with a blue crayon, the broken midline with blue, and the baseline with red. (visual, kinesthetic)

Stop and Check

You will see stop and check signs in your book when you finish a line of writing. When you see this sign, stop and circle the best letter you wrote on that line.

Circle the best letter on this line.

a a a *a* ✓

Keys to Legibility

There are four kinds of keys in your book. The words on the keys are **Shape, Size, Spacing,** and **Slant**. Good writers think about these things when they write.

The keys will help you make sure your writing is legible. **Legible** means easy to read.

13

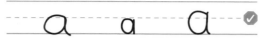

auditory   visual   kinesthetic

✓ **Stop and Check** Direct children to look at the photograph of the child holding a red stop sign with a check mark in it on student page 13. Explain that this sign means they are to stop and circle the best letter they wrote on that line. Guide children in evaluating the letters on the student page by having them compare the letters with the models. Then have them circle the best letter on that line.

Note: The development of self-evaluation skills is an important goal of handwriting instruction. Self-evaluation helps children become independent learners and because it fosters legibility, it is a benefit in all the content areas.

Keys to Legibility

Have children look at the four keys pictured on student page 13. Point out that as they are learning to write, they will encounter one of these keys in every letter lesson. The words on the keys—**shape, size, spacing, slant**—direct them to look at and think about certain aspects of their writing, making sure it is legible, or easy to read.

Note: Ask the children to look through their book to find examples of the features and elements highlighted and described on student pages 12 and 13.

Fun With Guidelines

Draw guidelines with chalk on the playground hardtop or make them with masking tape on the floor. Ask volunteers to follow directions similar to these:

Hop along the headline.
Lie on the midline.
Sit on the baseline.
Sit in the space below the baseline.
Walk the baseline on tiptoes.

Invite children to say directions for classmates to follow.

The Keys to Legibility

Provide large pieces of brightly colored construction paper, one piece each of green, blue, purple, and red. Have groups of children choose one of the pieces and prepare a large Key shape. They should label their key with the appropriate word for their color (green—shape, blue—size, purple—spacing, red—slant). Display the finished Keys where they can be handy reminders of legibility as the children write.

T13

Sing "The Alphabet Song," replacing the last two lines with the following.

> **When you see the ABC's, Look for some straight lines with me.**

Ask children to tell what kind of line is mentioned.

Tell children they will be looking for lines that are straight up and down. Explain that straight up and down lines are vertical lines. Ask children to stand up straight. Point out that a vertical line might be drawn from the top of their heads to the bottom of their feet or from their feet to the top of their heads.

Basic Strokes
Vertical Lines

Some letters and numerals have lines that are straight up and down.

Trace the straight up and down lines in these letters and numerals.

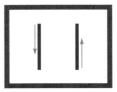

H D E t b i 9 4

Start at the green dot. ●
Trace the vertical lines.

14

1. Present the Lines

Direct the children to look at the letters and numerals on student page 14. Ask them to think about vertical lines and to tell what they see in these examples. (*There is at least one vertical line in each.*)

Model Model forming vertical lines in the air. Begin some at the top, and say, "Pull down straight." Begin others at the bottom, saying "Push up straight." Have the children repeat your words and follow the same actions.

Practice Have the children trace the vertical lines in the letters and numerals with an index finger, crayon, or pencil.

2. Trace the Lines

Ask the children to trace the vertical lines in the illustration on student page 14, remembering to begin each one at the green starting dot.

Encourage children to say, "Pull down straight" or "Push up straight" as they trace some of the lines.

Corrective Strategy

To help children write a vertical line, check the paper position. Help them practice pulling their index finger straight down from the headline to the baseline. Place a dot for start and a dot for stop, if needed. Say, "Pull down straight" as the children write.

Start at the green dot. •
Trace and write. Pull down straight.

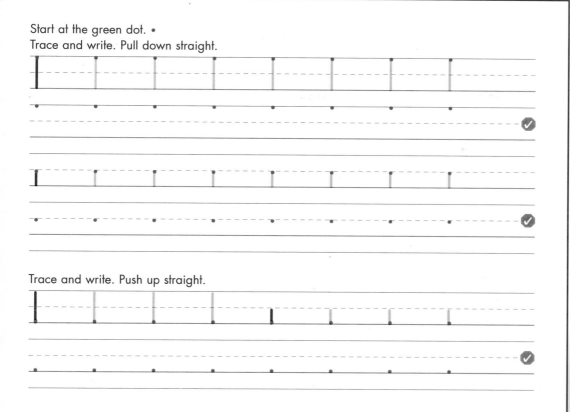

Trace and write. Push up straight.

15

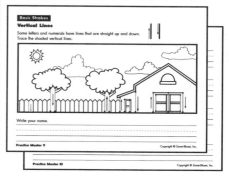

Fun and Games

auditory   visual   kinesthetic

Apply

Direct the children to trace the vertical lines, beginning each one at the proper starting point. Then have them write vertical lines of their own, again beginning each one at the green dot.

Stop and Check This icon directs the children to stop and circle their best vertical line. *(See page T13.)*

To help children evaluate, ask:
- Does each vertical line begin at the green dot?
- Did you trace a row of tall lines and a row of short lines?
- Do the vertical lines in your last row begin at the baseline?
- Are your vertical lines straight up and down?

Coaching Hint

Vertical Lines Have children look around the room for objects formed with lines. Help them determine whether a line is straight up and down and describe it using the term *vertical*. If possible, have them trace the lines as well. (visual, kinesthetic)

Lines, Lines, Lines

Distribute drawing paper and ask children to draw a picture somewhat like the picture on page 14 in their books, emphasizing vertical lines. Provide crayons, markers, colored chalk, or paint. Have children discuss their lines with a partner and circle their longest and shortest lines. Encourage them to count the number of lines of a certain color and the total number of lines.

What's in a Name?

Invite children to write their first name on the chalkboard. Then encourage them to take turns finding vertical lines in the letters in each other's names. Provide colored chalk, and have them highlight vertical lines they see.

Sing "The Alphabet Song," replacing the last two lines with the following.

> **When you see the ABC's, Look for some straight lines with me.**

Ask children to tell what kind of line is mentioned.

Tell children that now they will be looking for slide lines that go straight across. Explain that straight across lines are horizontal lines. Ask children to stand with arms outstretched. Point out that a horizontal line might be drawn from one hand to the other.

Basic Strokes
Horizontal Lines

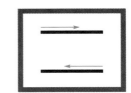

Some letters and numerals have slide lines.

Trace the slide lines in these letters and numerals.

F G B z f e 5 7

Start at the green dot. ●
Trace the slide lines.

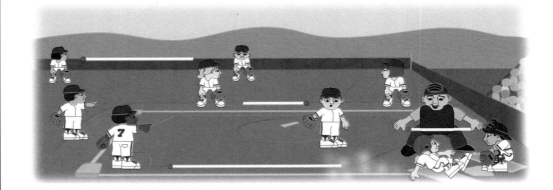

16

Present the Lines

Direct the children to look at the letters and numerals on student page 16. Ask them to think about horizontal lines and to tell what they see in these examples. (*There is at least one horizontal line in each.*)

Model Model forming horizontal lines in the air. Begin some at the left, and say, "Slide right." Begin others at the right, saying "Slide left." Have the children repeat your words and follow the same actions.

Practice Have the children trace the horizontal lines in the letters and numerals with an index finger, crayon, or pencil.

Trace the Lines

Ask the children to trace the horizontal lines in the illustration on student page 16, remembering to begin each one at the green starting dot.

Encourage children to say, "Slide right" or "Slide left" as they trace some of the lines.

Corrective Strategy

Help the children practice moving their index finger straight from left to right and straight from right to left. Place a dot for start and a dot for stop, if needed. Say, "Slide straight left" or "Slide straight right" as the children write.

Start at the green dot. •
Trace and write. Slide right.

Trace and write. Slide left.

17

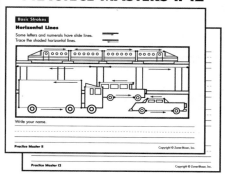

Basic Strokes
Horizontal Lines
Some letters and numerals have slide lines.
Trace the shaded horizontal lines.

Write your name.

Practice Master 11   Copyright © Zaner-Bloser, Inc.

Practice Master 12   Copyright © Zaner-Bloser, Inc.

Fun and Games

 auditory   visual   kinesthetic

Apply

Direct the children to trace the horizontal lines on student page 17, beginning each one at the green dot. Then have them write horizontal lines of their own, again beginning each one at the correct starting point.

Stop and Check This icon directs the children to stop and circle their best horizontal line. *(See page T13.)*

To help children evaluate, ask:
• Does each horizontal line begin at the green dot?
• Did you trace and write horizontal lines on the headline? The midline? The baseline?
• Do the horizontal lines in your last row slide toward the left?
• Are your horizontal lines straight across?

Coaching Hint

Horizontal Lines Have children look around the room for objects formed with lines. Help them determine whether a line is straight across and describe it using the term *horizontal*. If possible, have them trace the lines as well. (visual, kinesthetic)

Craft Stick Letters

Distribute craft sticks, glue, and construction paper for children to use to make letters. Ask children which letters have only vertical and horizontal lines (**E, F, H, I, L, l, T, t**) and write these letters on the chalkboard. Demonstrate how to place the sticks on construction paper to form a letter and then glue it in place. Have children share their completed letters.

What's in a Name?

Invite children to write their first name on the chalkboard. Then encourage them to take turns finding horizontal AND vertical lines in the letters in each other's names. Provide colored chalk, and have them highlight the horizontal and vertical lines they see.

T17

Sing "The Alphabet Song," replacing the last two lines with the following.

When you see the ABC's, Look for circle lines with me.

Ask children to tell what kind of line is mentioned.

Draw two circles on the chalkboard. Show where a backward circle line begins by marking a starting place, at about one o'clock, with a star. Ask children to begin at the star and use their index finger to trace over the line.

Show where a forward circle line begins by marking a starting place, at about nine o'clock, with a star. Ask children to begin at the star and use their index finger to trace over the line.

Basic Strokes
Backward Circle Lines

Some letters and numerals have backward circle lines.

Trace the backward circle lines in these letters and numerals.

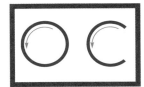

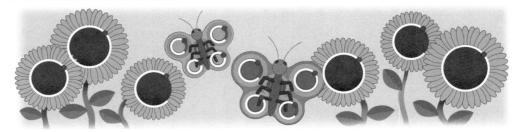

Start at the green dot. ●
Trace the backward circle lines.

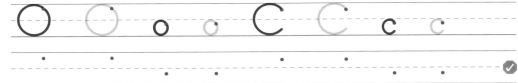

Trace and write. Circle back.

18

---

1 Present the Lines

Direct the children to look at the letters and numeral on student page 18. Ask them to think about circle lines and to tell what they see in these examples. (*There is a curved or circle line in each.*)

Model Use your arm to model making backward circles (left) and have the children copy you.

Practice Have the children use their index finger, a crayon, or a pencil to trace the backward circle lines in the letters and numerals. Some children will need help with direction.

2 Trace the Lines

Ask the children to trace the backward circle lines in the illustration on student page 18, remembering to begin each one at the green starting dot.

Encourage children to say, "Circle back" as they trace some of the lines.

Direct the children to trace the backward circle lines, on student page 18, beginning each one at the proper starting point. Then have them write backward circle lines of their own, again beginning each one at the green dot.

Repeat the teaching steps 1 and 2 for forward circle lines on student page 19.

✓ **Stop and Check** This icon directs the children to stop and circle their best circle line. (*See page T13.*)

To help children evaluate their backward and forward circles, ask:

- Does each circle or curve line begin at the green dot?
- Do your short circle and curve lines touch the midline and the baseline?
- Do your tall circle and curve lines touch the headline and the baseline?
- Are your circle and curve lines round?

Basic Strokes
Forward Circle Lines

Some letters and numerals have forward circle lines.

Trace the forward circle lines in these letters and numerals.

R P D b 5 3

Start at the green dot. ●
Trace the forward circle lines.

Trace and write. Circle forward.

19

Basic Strokes
Backward Circle Lines
Some letters and numerals have backward circle lines.
Trace the shaded backward circle lines.

Start at the dot. Trace and write. Circle back.

Write your name.

Fun and Games

auditory   visual   kinesthetic

Circles Are Round

Draw a large circle on a sheet of paper. Put a star for the start and an arrow pointing a direction for cutting. Duplicate a circle for each child. Have children help each other cut out the circles. Talk about things that are round, and ask children to draw round things on their circles.

Circle Left, Circle Right

Invite children to join hands and form a circle. Review that a circle can go backward, to the left, or forward, to the right. Play some music and have children move in a circle. Stop the music and have them change direction. Then chant this rhyme as you lead children in following the words and circling around.

> **Circle left, circle left.**
> **Circle all around.**
> **Circle right, circle right.**
> **Stop and look around.**

Corrective Strategy

To help children write a circle line, check the paper position. Help them practice moving their index finger in a round backward (left) or forward (right) circle movement. Place a dot for start and include an arrow, if needed. Say, "Circle back" or "Circle forward" as the children write.

Note: Use your arm to model making backward circles (left) and forward circles (right) and have children copy you.

Coaching Hint

Tracing Lines Use an overhead projector to project vertical, horizontal, and circle lines on the chalkboard. Ask children to wet their fingers in a cup of water and trace the enlarged lines on the chalkboard. (visual, kinesthetic)

Sing "The Alphabet Song," replacing the last two lines with the following.

When you see the ABC's, Look for some slant lines with me.

Ask children to tell what kind of line is mentioned.

Give each child a craft stick. Ask children to make the stick stand straight up and down (vertical) and then to lie straight across (horizontal). Demonstrate how to make the stick slant right, then left. Ask children to copy you. Explain that they will be looking for lines that slant right or left.

Basic Strokes
Slant Lines

Some letters and numerals have slant lines.

Trace the slant lines in these letters and numerals.

A N Q y w z 2 7

Start at the green dot. ●
Trace the slant lines.

20

---

1. Present the Lines

Direct the children to look at the letters and numerals on student page 20. Ask them to think about slant lines and to tell what they see in these examples. (*There is at least one slant line in each.*)

Model Model in the air a line that slants right and then a line that slants left and have the children copy you. Next have them imitate as you make an **X** to show a letter that has both a slant right and a slant left line.

Practice Have the children use their index finger, a crayon, or a pencil to trace the slant lines in the letters and numerals.

2. Trace the Lines

Ask the children to trace the slant lines in the illustration, remembering to begin each one at the green starting dot.

Encourage children to say, "Slant left," "Slant right," or "Slant up" as they trace some of the lines.

Corrective Strategy

To help children write a slant line, check the paper position. Help them practice moving their index finger from the headline, down toward the left, to the baseline (slant left); from the headline, down toward the right, to the baseline (slant right); or from the baseline, up toward the right, to the headline (slant up). Place a dot for start and include an arrow, if needed. Say, "Slant left," "Slant right," or "Slant up" as the children write.

Start at the green dot. •
Trace and write. Slant right.

Trace and write. Slant left.

Trace and write. Slant up.

21

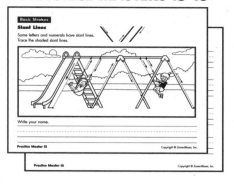

Fun and Games

auditory   visual   kinesthetic

Apply

Direct the children to trace the slant lines on student page 21, beginning each one at the green dot. Then have them write slant lines of their own, again beginning each one at the correct point.

Stop and Check This icon directs the children to stop and circle their best slant line. *(See page T13.)*

To help children evaluate, ask:
- Does each slant line begin at the green dot?
- Do your short slant lines touch the midline and the baseline?
- Do your tall slant lines touch the headline and the baseline?
- Are your slant lines straight?

Coaching Hint

Tracing Lines On guidelines on the chalkboard, write several slant lines, including slant left, slant right, and slant up lines, both tall and short. Encourage volunteers to identify and trace with colored chalk the kind of line you call out. (visual, kinesthetic)

Crazy Critters Have children use circle and slant strokes to draw pictures of insects or animals. Caterpillars and bees are possible suggestions to get them started.

Chalkboard Drawing Have children take turns at the chalkboard as you give these directions for drawing a house.

Make the outside walls with vertical lines.

Make the floor with a horizontal line.

Make the windows with horizontal and circle lines.

Make the roof with slant lines, left and right.

Make the bushes with backward and forward circles.

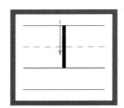

Touch the headline; **pull down straight** to the baseline.

Touch below the headline; **curve forward** (right); **slant left** to the baseline. **Slide right**.

Writing Numerals

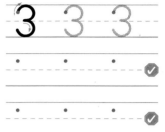

Trace and write.

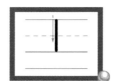

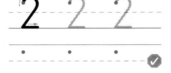

Stroke descriptions to guide numeral formation at home:

| Pull down straight. | Curve forward; slant left. Slide right. | Curve forward. Curve forward. |

1. Present the Numerals

Direct the children to look at the model of the numeral **1**. Ask them to tell what it looks like. *(a vertical line; a lowercase l)*

Model Write **1** on guidelines as you say the stroke description. Model writing **1** in the air as you repeat the stroke description. Have the children say it as they write **1** in the air with you.

Practice Let the children practice writing the numeral on marker boards or slates or on other paper before they write on the page.

2. Write and Evaluate

Ask the children to trace the shaded numerals with pencil, beginning each one at the dot. Then ask them to write the rows of **1**'s.

Stop and Check This icon directs children to stop and circle their best numeral.

To help them evaluate **1,** ask:
- Is the pull down straight stroke in your **1** straight?
- Does your **1** touch both the headline and the baseline?

Repeat teaching steps 1 and 2 for numerals 2, 3, 4, and 5.

To help children evaluate **2, 3, 4,** and **5,** ask:
- Does your **2** begin below the headline?

- Does the slide right stroke in your **2** rest on the baseline?
- Are both parts of your **3** about the same size?
- Does your **3** touch the headline and the baseline?
- Do both pull down straight strokes in your **4** touch the headline?
- Is the slide right stroke in your **4** on the midline?
- Is the slide right stroke in your **5** on the headline?
- Does your **5** rest on the base-line?

T22

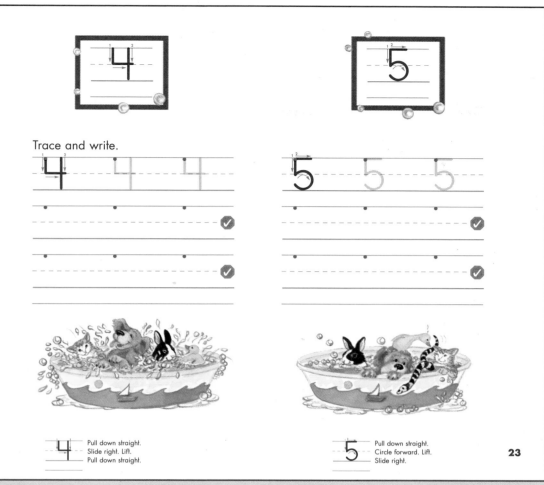

Trace and write.

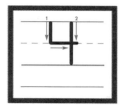

3

Touch below the headline; **curve forward** (right) to the midline; **curve forward** (right), ending above the baseline.

4

Touch the headline; **pull down straight** to the midline. **Slide right**. Lift. Move to the right and touch the headline; **pull down straight** to the baseline.

5

Touch the headline; **pull down straight** to the midline. **Circle forward** (right), ending above the baseline. Lift. Touch the headline; **slide right**.

23

Corrective Strategies

To help children write **2** correctly, point out that the slide right stroke that ends the numeral must be written on the baseline. There is no loop between the slant left and slide right strokes.

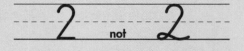

To help children write **4** correctly, explain that although they do not lift the pencil at the end of the first pull down straight stroke, they should still stop and then slide right.

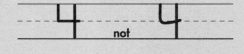

PRACTICE MASTERS 18–20

Numerals 1–2
Trace and write 1.

Trace and write 2.

2 2 2 2 2 2 2

Write your name.

Practice Master 18   Copyright © Zaner-Bloser, Inc.

Practice Master 19   Copyright © Zaner-Bloser, Inc.

Practice Master 20   Copyright © Zaner-Bloser, Inc.

Coaching Hint

Lined or Unlined? Children vary in their ability to write within the confines of a designated area. Some children may not be ready to use lined paper. The teacher should decide what type of paper is best for individuals.

Fun and Games

| auditory | visual | kinesthetic |

Number Chart Cut colored paper into one-inch squares. Have the children write the numerals **1** through **5** down the left side of their paper. Invite them to paste squares in rows going across—one square next to **1**, two squares next to **2**, and so on. Review the completed charts together.

T23

Touch the headline; **curve down** to the baseline. **Curve up** to the midline and around to close the circle.

Touch the headline; **slide right**. **Slant left** to the baseline.

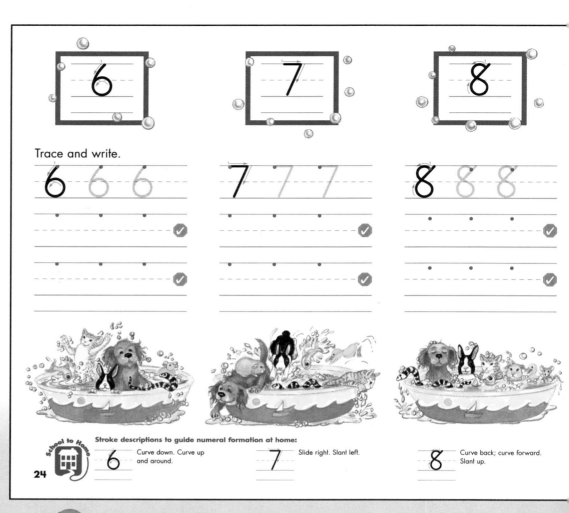

Trace and write.

6 6 6   7 7 7   8 8 8

Stroke descriptions to guide numeral formation at home:

6 — Curve down. Curve up and around.

7 — Slide right. Slant left.

8 — Curve back; curve forward. Slant up.

24

1. Present the Numerals

Direct the children to look at the model of the numeral **6**. Ask them to tell where **6** begins (*at the headline*) and where it ends (*below the midline*).

Model Write **6** on guidelines as you say the stroke description. Model writing **6** in the air as you repeat the stroke description. Have the children use their index finger to write **6** on their desktop as you say the description again.

Practice Let the children practice writing the numeral on marker boards or slates or on other paper before they write on the page.

2. Write and Evaluate

Ask the children to trace the shaded numerals with pencil, beginning each one at the dot. Then ask them to write the rows of **6**'s.

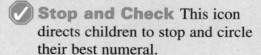 **Stop and Check** This icon directs children to stop and circle their best numeral.

To help them evaluate **6,** ask:
- Does your **6** begin at the headline with a curve down stroke?
- Does your **6** have a closed circle?
- Does your **6** touch both the headline and the baseline?

Repeat teaching steps 1 and 2 for numerals 7, 8, 9, and 10.

To help students evaluate **7, 8, 9,** and **10,** ask:
- Does your **7** begin on the headline and end on the baseline?

- Is the slide right stroke in your **7** written on the headline?
- Does the slant stroke in your **8** connect with the beginning stroke?
- Are the curves of your **8** about the same size?
- Does your **9** have a round backward circle?
- Is your **9** straight up and down?
- Is there a space between **1** and **0** in your **10**?
- Does your **10** touch the headline and the baseline?

T24

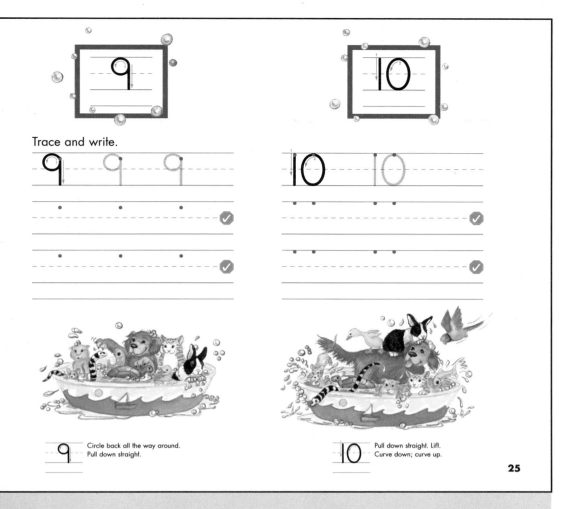

Trace and write.

9 9 9
10 10

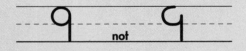
9 Circle back all the way around. Pull down straight.

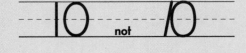
10 Pull down straight. Lift. Curve down; curve up.

25

Touch below the headline; **curve back** (left); **curve forward** (right), touching the baseline; **slant up** (right) to the headline.

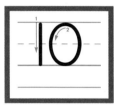

Touch below the headline; **circle back** (left) all the way around. **Pull down straight** to the baseline.

Touch the headline; **pull down straight** to the baseline. Lift. Touch the headline; **curve down** to the baseline; **curve up** to the headline.

Corrective Strategies

To help children write **9** correctly, remind them to make a complete backward circle so no gap remains between the beginning and ending strokes.

9 not 9

To help children write **10** correctly, explain that they must write the numerals straight up and down and remember to leave a space between them.

10 not 10

PRACTICE MASTERS 21–22

Numerals 7–8
Trace and write 7.
7 7 7 7
Trace and write 8.
8 8 8 8 8 8
Write your name.
Practice Master 21   Copyright © Zaner-Bloser, Inc.
Practice Master 22   Copyright © Zaner-Bloser, Inc.

Coaching Hint

Name That Numeral For children having difficulty forming their numerals correctly, place on the chalk ledge a set of raised numerals made of seeds or sandpaper. Name a numeral. Have children take turns tracing the numeral several times as you say the stroke description. (kinesthetic)

Fun and Games

auditory   visual   kinesthetic

Count and Write

Prepare squares of paper with or without guidelines. Pair children and tell one child to arrange small objects such as blocks, buttons, or seeds into a group. Ask the other child to write the numeral that shows how many. Have children exchange tasks.

Practice

Practice

Write **1 – 5**.

1   2   3   4   5

On Your Own

Write a numeral. Draw a picture to show how many.

26

---

1 Review the Numerals

Direct the children to look at the numerals on the page. Ask them what they remember about how to write these numerals. *(All are tall, reaching from the headline to the baseline; all are written straight up and down.)*

Review the stroke descriptions and model again any of the numerals the children may be having difficulty writing.

Ask a volunteer to give a verbal description of one of these numerals: **1, 2, 3, 4, 5**. Challenge the other children to identify the numeral being described and then write it on guidelines on the chalkboard.

2 Write and Evaluate

Direct the children to write the numerals, beginning each one at the proper starting point. Remind children to form their numerals carefully so they will be easy to read. Then have them respond to **On Your Own**.

✓ **Stop and Check** To help children evaluate their numerals **1–5**, ask:

- Does your **1** begin at the headline and end at the baseline, and is it a straight stroke?
- Does the curve forward stroke of your **2** touch the headline?
- Do the curve forward strokes of your **3** end and begin at the midline?
- Is the slide right stroke of your **4** on the midline?
- Does the circle forward stroke of your **5** go slightly above the midline before circling down?

To help children evaluate their numerals **6–10**, ask:

- Does the curved ending of your **6** touch the midline?
- Is the slide right stroke of your **7** on the headline?
- Does the slant up stroke of your **8** touch the beginning stroke?
- Does the circle back stroke of your **9** make a complete circle?
- Did you touch the headline and baseline both times in your **10**?

Corrective Strategies

To help the children write **3**, give them a correct model of the numeral to trace over. Emphasize that the two rounded parts of **3** are about the same size.

3   *not*   3

T26

Write Away

Use Numerals

Brainstorm with the children and list places where they see numerals, such as on houses, calendars, highways, street signs, and book pages. Then discuss ways we use numerals. Duplicate sets of questions that can be answered with numerals. Have the children write the numeral that answers each question on paper with guidelines.

Questions might include these:

- How old are you?
- How many brothers do you have?
- What number is on your house or apartment?
- What day is your birthday?

Write **6 – 10**.

6   7   8   9   10

On Your Own

Write a numeral. Draw a picture to show how many.

27

To help the children write **5**, remind them to write the numeral straight up and down.

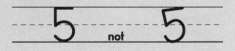
5 not 5

To help the children write **8**, point out that the numeral begins below the headline so the final stroke can connect with it.

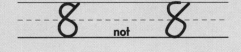
8 not 8

PRACTICE MASTER 75

Numeral Practice

Write 1–5.

1   2   3   4   5

Write 6–10.

6   7   8   9   10

Write the number sentence.

1 + 3 = 4

Copyright © Zaner-Bloser, Inc.   Practice Master 75

Coaching Hint

Using Guidelines As you demonstrate on the chalkboard, have the children do the following on paper with guidelines.

- Draw over the baseline with red crayon.
- Draw over the headline with blue crayon.
- Draw over the midline with blue crayon.

(visual, kinesthetic)

T27

Just How Many? On chart paper, list the names of objects in your classroom, leaving a space before each word for a child to write a numeral. For example, _____ *chairs*. Have each child choose a word, count the number of those items they see, and fill in the blank space. Read the chart together.

Application

Write the number sentences.

 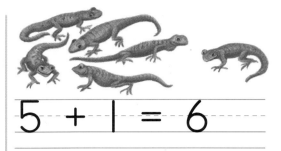

$$1 + 2 = 3 \qquad 5 + 1 = 6$$

$$+ \quad =$$

$$7 + 2 = 9 \qquad 4 + 4 = 8$$

$$+ \quad = \qquad + \quad =$$

28

1. Review the Numerals

Direct the children to look at the numerals on the page. Encourage volunteers to select a numeral of their choice and say the stroke description for forming that numeral. Point out that the numerals on these two pages are written in number sentences that show addition or subtraction.

If children are still having difficulty forming a specific numeral, repeat the modeling process for that numeral. Write the numeral on guidelines on the chalkboard as you say the stroke description. Then model writing the numeral in the air as you repeat the stroke description. Have the children say it as they write the numeral in the air with you.

2. Write and Evaluate

After the children have practiced writing several of the numerals on marker boards or slates or on other paper, direct them to write the first row of number sentences on the page. Point out that the function symbols are already written for them.

 Stop and Check To help students evaluate their numerals, ask:

- Are your numerals straight up and down?
- Do your numerals all touch both the headline and the baseline?
- Are your straight strokes straight and even?
- Are your circle and curve strokes rounded?

Write the number sentences.

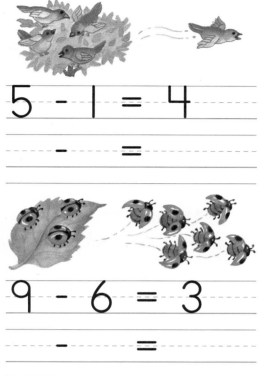

$$5 - 1 = 4$$
$$\_\_ - \_\_ = \_\_$$

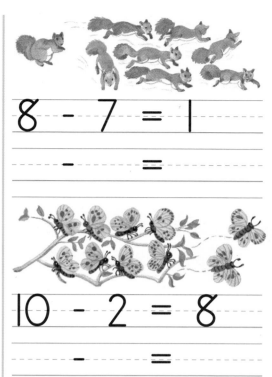

$$8 - 7 = 1$$
$$\_\_ - \_\_ = \_\_$$

$$9 - 6 = 3$$
$$\_\_ - \_\_ = \_\_$$

$$10 - 2 = 8$$
$$\_\_ - \_\_ = \_\_$$

29

Apply

Ask the children to complete the pages by writing the numerals that complete each number sentence. Remind them to write their numerals carefully and to refer back to the models if they need help remembering the correct forms.

After the children have completed the page and evaluated their writing, have them write a numeral on a piece of newsprint or other drawing paper. Then have them illustrate their chosen numeral by drawing something that shows that value.

Coaching Hint

Basic Strokes Provide large sheets of newsprint and a dark crayon for each child. Let the children tape their papers to a chalkboard or wall and practice their strokes in large, sweeping motions. Encourage them to practice each stroke several times and to feel the motion that each one involves. (kinesthetic, visual)

How Many of What?
Encourage the children to imagine they are in charge of a certain part of a grocery store or a toy store. Provide newsprint or other drawing paper, and direct the children to fold the paper in half longwise once. Have them write a numeral (from 1 to 10) on the left-hand side of the paper and then draw that number of specific items on the right-hand side. They might choose apples, canned foods, bakery items, beach balls, toy trucks, etc.

Straight or Curly? Write the numerals 1–10 in a large size on the chalkboard or on a large piece of chart paper. Invite the children to help you classify the numerals according to their basic shapes. Ask questions such as these:

- Which numerals are made with all straight lines? (**1, 4, 7**)
- Which numerals are made with some straight lines and some curved lines? (**2, 5, 9, 10**)
- Which numerals are made with all curved lines? (**3, 6, 8**)

Invite the children to tell ways numerals can be shown made with all straight lines (*digital clocks, some advertising signs, some computer games, special effects, etc.*) or with all curved lines (*art, advertising signs, etc.*).

Featured Letters

IL iI tT
oO aA dD

Featured Key to Legibility:

Shape

The basic strokes—vertical, horizontal, circle, slant—written correctly in specific combinations yield letters with correct shape. Children will learn to look at letter shape as they evaluate their writing.

Other Acceptable Letterforms

The following letterforms are acceptable variations of the models shown in this book.

t t A

Alternate Letter Formation

Use these stroke descriptions to show an alternate method for children who have difficulty using the continuous-stroke method.

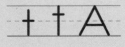

a **Circle back** all the way around. Lift.
Pull down straight.

d **Circle back** all the way around. Lift.
Pull down straight.

Keys to Legibility

Make your writing easy to read. Look at the shape of each letter.

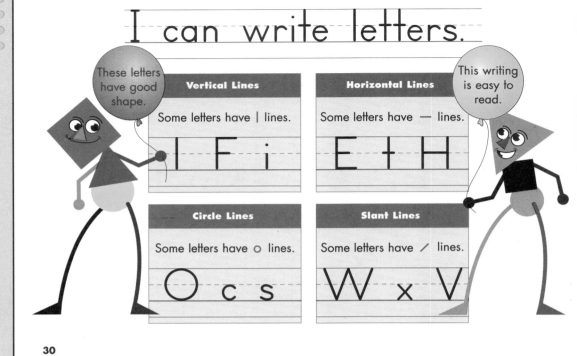

Shape

I can write letters.

These letters have good shape.

This writing is easy to read.

Vertical Lines
Some letters have | lines.
I F i

Horizontal Lines
Some letters have — lines.
E t H

Circle Lines
Some letters have o lines.
O c s

Slant Lines
Some letters have / lines.
W x V

30

---

1. Present the Key

Point out the Key feature on student page 30. Explain to children that they will see this feature often. It directs them to consider certain aspects of their writing to determine which letter is written best.

Ask the children to look at the cartoon characters on the page and to name or describe shapes they see in the figures. Point out that the letters they are learning to write have special shapes, too.

Write on the chalkboard several examples of the strokes shown on the page. Invite volunteers to come to the chalkboard and write lines that you name—*vertical, horizontal, circle,* and *slant*. Point out that all the lowercase and uppercase letters are made with these lines, or strokes.

2. Trace and Evaluate

Read the directions for the first row of letters on student page 31. Encourage the children to trace all the vertical lines they see in these letters. Then have them continue in the same way, tracing each kind of line shown in the remaining three rows of letters.

Write letters from the page on guidelines on the chalkboard. Have volunteers come to the board and use chalk of different colors to trace examples of the kinds of lines you call out. Guide the children in evaluating the quality of the traced lines, noticing details such as straightness, correct slant, and smooth curve.

Trace the | lines in these letters.

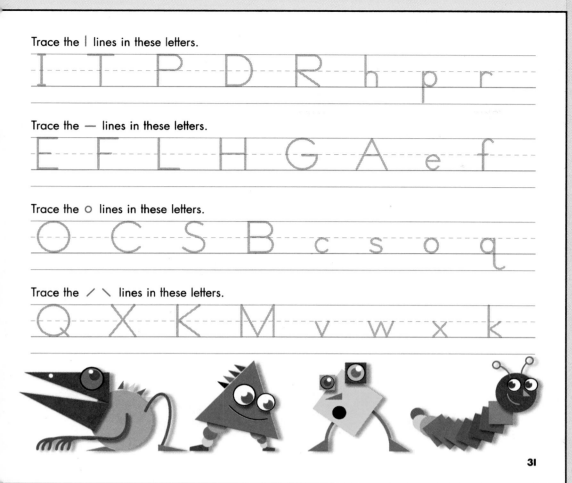

I T P D R h p r

Trace the — lines in these letters.

E F L H G A e f

Trace the O lines in these letters.

O C S B c s o q

Trace the / \ lines in these letters.

Q X K M v w x k

31

Teaching the Letters:
Building Imagery

The purpose of the first step in teaching each letter is to help the children develop a clear **mental image** of the letter to be written. Appropriate questions about the letter are included to help the children develop the image. The teacher is then asked to model, or demonstrate, the letter on the chalkboard, on large chart paper, or in the air, giving attention to the letter and its description, to establish **motor image**.

Meeting Individual Needs

for auditory learners
As you say the specific strokes for a letter, have the children write that letter.

for visual learners
Encourage the children to look closely at the individual strokes within a certain letter and to compare that letter with other similar letters before they begin to write it.

for kinesthetic learners
Have the children use full-arm movement to write large letters in the air.

What the research says . . .

Solid familiarity with the visual shapes of the individual letters is an absolute prerequisite for learning to read.
—Marilyn Jager Adams, *Beginning to Read: Thinking and Learning About Print.* © Massachusetts Institute of Technology

Note: As the children are learning to print, take the time to strengthen the reading/writing connection by focusing on the unique shapes and attributes of each letter.

Support Materials

These support products and materials for the beginning writer are available in the **Handwriting** section of the Zaner-Bloser catalog.

- *Touch and Trace Letter Cards*
- *Now I Know My ABCs (a multimodal kit-in-a-book)*
- *Fine Motor Development Kit*
- *Listening Alphabeat*
- *Write-On, Wipe-Off Practice Boards*
- *Tri-Go Pencil Grips*
- *Writing Frame*

See the **Keys to Legibility Poster** *for more information.*

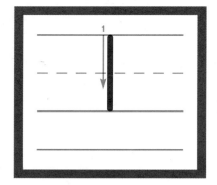

Touch the headline; **pull down straight** to the baseline.

Name: _____

Trace and write.

l l l l l l l

✓

✓

leaf   like

Trace and write.

L L L L L

✓

✓

Lola   Len

Stroke descriptions to guide letter formation at home:

l Pull down straight.

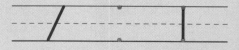
L Pull down straight.
Slide right.

---

1. Present the Letter

Direct the children to look at lowercase **l**. Focus attention on the letter's shape by asking them to name things in the classroom that look like the letter **l**.

Model Write **l** on guidelines as you say the stroke description. Model writing **l** in the air as you repeat the stroke description. Have the children say it as they write **l** in the air with you.

Practice Let the children practice writing **l** on marker boards or slates or on other paper before they write on the pages.

Note: As children write on the student pages, remember to focus on the letter being taught on that page. Children are not expected to master letters not yet introduced.

2. Write and Evaluate

Ask the children to trace the shaded letters with pencil, beginning each one at the dot. Then ask them to carefully write two rows of letters and the words with **l**.

✓ **Stop and Check** This icon directs children to stop and circle their best letter. (*See p. T13.*)

To help them evaluate **l**, ask:
- Does your **l** begin at the headline?
- Is your **l** straight up and down?

Repeat teaching steps 1 and 2 for uppercase L.

To help children evaluate **L**, ask:
- Does your **L** stop at the baseline before the slide right stroke?
- Is your slide right stroke on the baseline?

Corrective Strategy

To help the children write a vertical **l**, check the paper position. Help them practice pulling the index finger straight down from the headline to the baseline. Place a dot for *start* and a dot for *stop*. Say the stroke description as the children write **l**.

Families may use the stroke descriptions on the student page to encourage good letter formation at home. Copy and distribute **Practice Master 84** for children to take home for more practice.

Write the words.

lemon   lake   live   love

Write the sentence.

Look at my letters.

On Your Own   Write words to finish the sentence.

My letters are

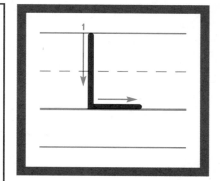

Touch the headline; **pull down straight** to the baseline. **Slide right.**

Shape

Circle your best letter that has a **l** line.

33

---

auditory   visual   kinesthetic

3 Apply

Before the children write the words and sentence, ask them to look at the page and identify letters with vertical, horizontal, and circle lines. Review the fact that **l** has a vertical line. **L** has one vertical and one horizontal line. Observe the children as they complete the page and respond to **On Your Own**.

Shape

Help the children evaluate the shape of the letters they wrote by comparing them with the models. Then have them respond to the directions in the Key feature at the bottom of the page.

PRACTICE MASTERS 23–24

Name:

Write the letter and the words.

tie   life   late   left

land   last   line   lunch

Copyright © Zaner-Bloser, Inc.   Practice Master 23

Lune lives in Lima.

Practice Master 24   Copyright © Zaner-Bloser, Inc.

Coaching Hint

Paper Position Correct paper placement will help children write with greater ease and legibility. Check this periodically with each child. Remind children to check their paper placement whenever they write. (Refer to the positions for writing on pages 10 and 11 in this Teacher Edition.)

Letter Hunt Hide letter cards around the classroom. Ask the children to go on a letter hunt as they sing "A-Hunting We Will Go." Have the children write the letters they find on the chalkboard and name a word that begins with the letter.

Vertical Lines Fill a learning center with a variety of ways for the children to practice the pull down straight stroke. Ideas may include using their fingers to trace a craft stick from top to bottom, pulling a zipper down, and painting pull down straight "raindrops" on an easel.

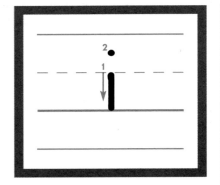

Touch the midline; **pull down straight** to the baseline. Lift. **Dot**.

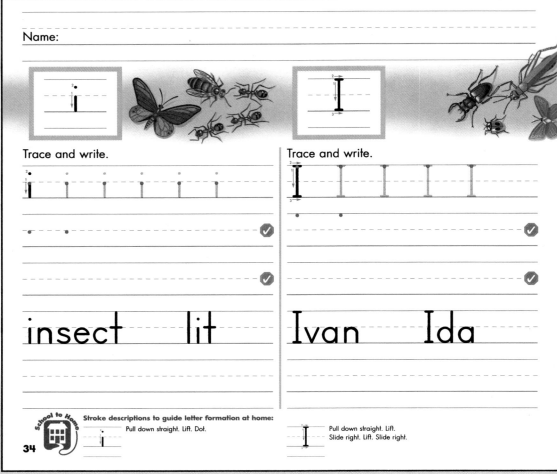

Name: _____

Trace and write.

insect   lit

Trace and write.

Ivan   Ida

School to Home Stroke descriptions to guide letter formation at home:

i — Pull down straight. Lift. Dot.

I — Pull down straight. Lift. Slide right. Lift. Slide right.

---

1. Present the Letter

Have the children look at lowercase **i**. Ask volunteers to describe how the letter is formed and where to place the dot.

Model Write **i** on guidelines as you say the stroke description. Invite the children to write **i** on their desktop with their index finger. Have them say the description with you as they write.

Practice Let the children practice writing **i** on marker boards or slates or on other paper before they write on the pages.

2. Write and Evaluate

Ask the children to trace the shaded letters with pencil, beginning each one at the green starting dot. Then tell them to write two rows of letters and the words with **i**.

✓ **Stop and Check** This icon directs children to stop and circle their best letter. (*See p. T13.*)

To help them evaluate **i,** ask:
- Is your **i** resting on the baseline?
- Is your letter straight up and down?

*Repeat teaching steps 1 and 2 for uppercase **I**.*

To help children evaluate **I,** ask:
- Does your **I** begin at the headline?
- Is your **I** about the same width as the model?

Corrective Strategy

To help the children write the slide right strokes of **I** the correct width, have them trace the pull down straight stroke and then connect dots placed at appropriate widths on the headline and baseline. Say the description as they write **I**.

School to Home

Families may use the stroke descriptions on the student page to encourage good letter formation at home. Copy and distribute **Practice Master 85** for children to take home for more practice.

T34

Write the words.

inch   ill   into   it

Write the sentence.

I like to write my name.

On Your Own Write words to finish the sentence.

I really like

Shape
Circle your best letter that has a I line.

35

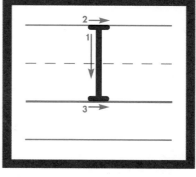

Touch the headline; **pull down straight** to the baseline. Lift. Touch the headline; **slide right**. Lift. Touch the baseline; **slide right**.

Fun and Games

auditory   visual   kinesthetic

3 Apply

Remind the children to think about shape as they write, remembering to make strokes as straight as possible. Observe the children as they complete the page and respond to **On Your Own**.

Shape

Help the children evaluate the shape of the letters they wrote by comparing them with the models. Then have them respond to the directions in the Key feature at the bottom of the page.

PRACTICE MASTERS 25–26

Name:

Write the letter and the words.

i   i   i   i   i   i   i   i

if   idea   his   iron

is   inside   ice   in

Copyright © Zaner-Bloser, Inc.   Practice Master 25

Ira lives in Iowa.

Practice Master 26   Copyright © Zaner-Bloser, Inc.

Coaching Hint

Left-Handed Writers Any tendency to twist or "hook" the hand or wrist by the left-handed child should be corrected early. The twisting and turning are often attempts to see the paper, so correct paper position is vital.

I or i Game Write **I** and **i** on the chalkboard. Write all the children's names on index cards and place them in a bag. Choose one and ask whose name it is. Identify any **i** in the name. Ask the child to trace either **I** or **i** on the board. If the child traces **I**, he or she demonstrates an action for classmates to imitate. If the child traces **i**, he or she makes up a riddle about an animal or object for classmates to guess.

Writing Corner Paste one row of guidelines at the top of drawing paper. Have the children write *I like* on the lines. Then invite them to draw pictures of things, food, animals, or people they like. Suggest they talk in pairs or cooperative groups about the pictures.

T35

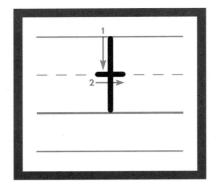

Touch the headline; **pull down straight** to the baseline. Lift. Touch the midline; **slide right**.

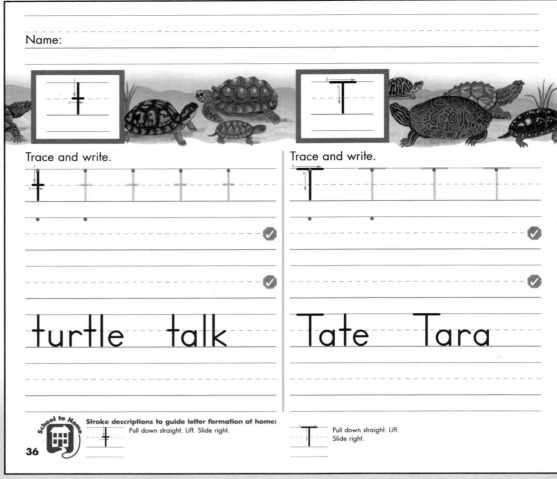

Name:

Trace and write.

Trace and write.

turtle talk

Tate Tara

36

1. Present the Letter

Have the children look at lowercase **t**. Help them recognize that the slide right stroke is on the midline.

Model Dip your index finger in a container of water and write **t** on guidelines on the chalkboard as you say the stroke description. Encourage the children to take turns dipping their finger in water and writing **t** on the chalkboard, repeating the stroke description with you as they write.

Practice Let the children practice writing **t** on marker boards or slates or on other paper before they write on the pages.

2. Write and Evaluate

Ask the children to trace the shaded letters with pencil, beginning each one at the dot. Then have them write two rows of letters and the words with **t**.

✓ **Stop and Check** This icon directs children to stop and circle their best letter. (*See p. T13.*)

To help them evaluate **t**, ask:
• Is your **t** straight up and down?
• Is the slide right stroke written on the midline?

*Repeat teaching steps 1 and 2 for uppercase **T**.*

To help children evaluate **T**, ask:
• Is your slide right stroke on the headline?
• Is your **T** about the same width as the model?

Corrective Strategy

To help the children avoid slanting **t**, remind them to shift the paper as the writing progresses. Have them practice pulling their index fingers straight down from the headline to the baseline before writing.

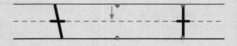

Write the words.

toy tub tell take

Write the sentence.

This is my toy train.

 On Your Own Write words to finish the sentence.

Toy trains are

 Shape
Circle your best letter
that has a — line.

37

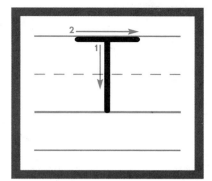

Touch the headline; **pull down straight** to the baseline. Lift. Touch the headline; **slide right**.

Fun and Games

auditory visual kinesthetic

Apply

Before the children write the words and sentence, ask them to look at the page and identify letters that are formed with straight lines. Remind them of the importance of using the guidelines as they form their letters. Observe the children as they complete the page and respond to **On Your Own**.

Shape

Help the children evaluate the shape of the letters they wrote by comparing them with the models. Then have them respond to the directions in the Key feature at the bottom of the page.

PRACTICE MASTERS 27–28

Name:

Write the letter and the words.

† † † † † † † † †

tail tie tree two

table tall tea teeth

Copyright © Zaner-Bloser, Inc. Practice Master 27

Tia met me in Texas.

Practice Master 28 Copyright © Zaner-Bloser, Inc.

Coaching Hint

Basic Strokes Have children look around the room for objects formed with lines. Help them determine whether a line is horizontal or vertical and describe it using the terms *pull down straight* or *slide right*. If possible, have them trace the lines as well. (visual, auditory, kinesthetic)

Color the Lines Choose different colors to represent vertical, horizontal, circle, and slant lines. Assign several uppercase and lowercase letters to each child. Invite children to write their letters on tagboard sheets, using crayons or markers of the selected colors. **T,** for example, would be written in two different colors: one for the vertical line and one for the horizontal line.

Jigsaw Puzzles Make jigsaw puzzles by writing each letterform on a square of tagboard and cutting it apart into its basic strokes. Invite the children to put the pieces together to practice correct letter shape.

Practice and Application

Practice

Write the letters.

l l l l l

i i i i i

t t t t t

L L L L

I I I I I

T T T T

Write the words.

it   lit   ill   till   little

38

1. Review the Letters

Direct the children to look at the letters being reviewed on student page 38. Ask them what they remember about the shape of these letters. *(All are made with straight lines.)*

Review the stroke descriptions and model again any of the letters the children may be having difficulty writing.

Ask a volunteer to give a verbal description of one of these letters: **l, i, t, L, I, T**. Challenge the other children to identify the letter being described and then write it on guidelines on the chalkboard.

2. Write and Evaluate

Tell the children to write the letters, beginning each one at the proper starting point. Then have them write the words on the page. Remind children to form their letters carefully so they will have correct shape and be easy to read.

Stop and Check

To help children evaluate their lowercase letters, ask:

- Does your **l** begin at the headline?
- Did you remember to dot your **i**?
- Is your **t** crossed on the midline?

To help children evaluate their uppercase letters, ask:

- Are the lines in your **L** straight?
- Do the slide right strokes in your **I** touch the headline and the baseline?
- Is your **T** about the same width as the model?

Corrective Strategy

To help the children write **I,** remind them that the slide right strokes are shorter than a similar stroke in **T.**

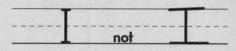

not

More About Practice

Because handwriting is a motor skill that becomes automatic over time, practice makes permanent, not necessarily perfect. Asking children to write letters many times without stopping to evaluate can reinforce bad habits and lead to sloppy, rushed work. Instead, have students write a letter several times and then circle their best attempt.

T38

Application Write the sentences.

Look at me!

Today is my birthday.

I am one year older.

My Words

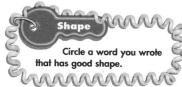
Shape

Circle a word you wrote
that has good shape.

39

Write Away

A Birthday Surprise
Invite children to help plan a surprise birthday party for a familiar storybook character. After they choose a character, help them develop two lists: one that includes the names of other characters to invite to the party and one that includes items needed for the party. Have children draw pictures to show the imaginary celebration.

3 Apply

Before children write the sentences on student page 39, ask volunteers to look at the page and identify strokes they recognize in the letters. Remind children to write their letters with proper shape so they will be easy to read. Observe children as they write on the page.

My Words Ask children to write birthday words of their own. Encourage them to write words that contain the review letters. If they need help, suggest they look for words on the previous pages.

Shape

Help children summarize what they have learned about shape. Then have them respond to the direction in the Key feature.

Special Helps

Providing a vertical surface, such as an easel or chalkboard, for handwriting practice will greatly benefit children who tend to bend and twist their wrists awkwardly when writing.

The vertical orientation straightens the wrist and increases the child's hand and fine motor function. The shoulder muscles, which are important in writing, are also strengthened.

—Maureen King, O.T.R.

Fun and Games

auditory   visual   kinesthetic

Letter Walk With masking tape, make a large **l** and **L** on the floor. Invite children to walk along the outline of the letters as you say directions for forming them. Then have the children jump, hop, or tiptoe along the letters. Repeat the procedure with **i** and **I** and with **t** and **T**.

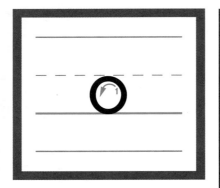

Touch below the midline; **circle back** (left) all the way around.

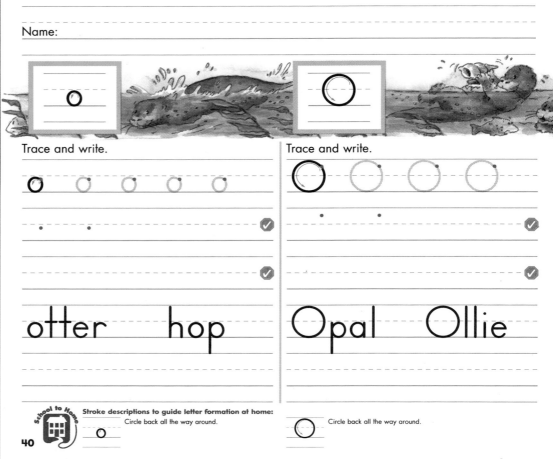

Name:

Trace and write.

Trace and write.

otter   hop

Opal Ollie

School to Home

40

Stroke descriptions to guide letter formation at home:
Circle back all the way around.

Circle back all the way around.

---

1. Present the Letter

Direct the children to look at lowercase **o**. Ask what things in the classroom are shaped like the letter **o**.

Model Write **o** on guidelines as you say the stroke description. Give each child a circular carton lid and have the children trace the outer edge of the lid with their finger as you say the description. Show them where to begin and in which direction to circle.

Practice Have the children practice writing **o** on marker boards or slates or on other paper before they write on the pages.

2. Write and Evaluate

Ask the children to trace the shaded letters with pencil, beginning each one at the dot. Then have them write two rows of letters and the words with **o**.

✓ **Stop and Check** This icon directs the children to stop and circle their best letter.

To help them evaluate **o**, ask:
• Is your **o** round?
• Does your **o** rest on the baseline?

*Repeat teaching steps 1 and 2 for uppercase **O**.*

To help children evaluate **O**, ask:
• Is your **O** closed properly?
• Is your **O** about the same width as the model?

Corrective Strategy

To help the children make a round **o**, have them use a template or trace around tagboard circles. On paper, place a dot for *start* and several other dots to form a circle. Ask the children to connect the dots by circling back (left) without lifting the pencil.

School to Home

Families may use the stroke descriptions on the student page to encourage good letter formation at home. Copy and distribute **Practice Master 87** for children to take home for more practice.

T40

Write the words.

octopus   off   on   odd

Write the sentence.

Our class took a trip.

On Your Own Write words to finish the sentence.

Our trip was

Shape
Circle your best letter
that has a O line.

41

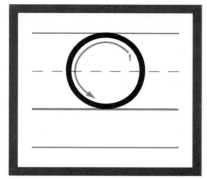

Touch below the headline;
circle back (left) all the way
around.

Fun and Games

auditory   visual   kinesthetic

Oo Collage Draw a bubble pipe on a large sheet of paper. Put it on the floor and let the children make bubbles. They can cut circular shapes from paper or fabric scraps and glue them to the collage. Cut handwriting paper into circles and have children write **O** and **o** on the guidelines. Add these bubbles to the collage, too.

Circle Back Game To help children understand circle back, have them join hands and circle left as they sing these words to the tune of "In and Out the Window."

Circle back around the classroom (Repeat twice more.)

And write O in the air.

(Children stop and in the air write **O**.)

Apply

Before the children write the words and sentence on the page, write *octopus* on guidelines on the chalkboard, making some obvious errors in how the letters are shaped. Invite the children to comment on whether this word is written correctly. Rewrite the word, pointing out that letters in a word must be the correct shape if they are to be easy to read. Observe the children as they complete the page and respond to **On Your Own**.

Shape

Help the children evaluate the shape of the letters they wrote by comparing them with the models. Then have them respond to the directions in the Key feature at the bottom of the page.

PRACTICE MASTERS 29–30

Name:

Write the letter and the words.

o o o o o o o o

oil   oat   only   other

one   old   out   over

Copyright © Zaner-Bloser, Inc.   Practice Master 29

Olive shops in Ohio.

Practice Master 30   Copyright © Zaner-Bloser, Inc.

Coaching Hint

To help children who make vertical, jagged lines when trying to write circles, provide small handfuls of clay and have the child roll them, one by one, between the curved palms to make smooth, meatball-like shapes. (kinesthetic)

Touch below the midline; **circle back** (left) all the way around. **Push up straight** to the midline. **Pull down straight** to the base-line.

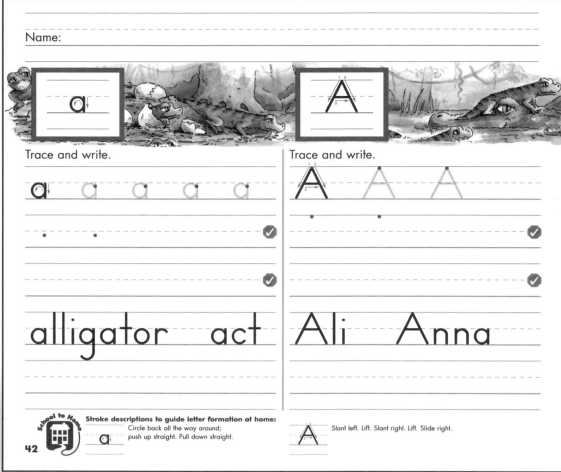

Name: _____

Trace and write.

a a a a a

· · ✓

✓

alligator act

Trace and write.

A A A A

· · ✓

✓

Ali Anna

Stroke descriptions to guide letter formation at home:
Circle back all the way around; push up straight. Pull down straight.

Slant left. Lift. Slant right. Lift. Slide right.

42

1. Present the Letter

Have the children look at lower-case **a.** Focus attention on the letter's shape by asking children what other letter they see in **a.**

Model Write **a** on guidelines as you say the stroke description. Model writing **a** in the air as you repeat the description. Have the children echo it as they write **a** in the air with you.

Practice Let the children practice writing **a** on marker boards or slates or on other paper before they write on the pages.

2. Write and Evaluate

Ask the children to trace the shaded letters with pencil, beginning each one at the dot. Then have the children write two rows of letters and the words with **a.**

 Stop and Check This icon directs the children to stop and circle their best letter.

To help them evaluate **a,** ask:
• Does your pull down straight stroke touch the circle?
• Does your **a** touch the midline?

Repeat teaching steps 1 and 2 for uppercase A.

To help children evaluate **A,** ask:
• Do your slant strokes touch the headline at the same spot?
• Is your slide right stroke on the midline?

Corrective Strategy

To help children write **A** the correct width, place two dots on the baseline and a dot on the head-line as shown. Have them con-nect the dots with slant left and slant right lines and make a slide right line on the midline.

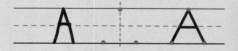

Families may use the stroke descriptions on the student page to encourage good letter formation at home. Copy and distribute **Practice Master 88** for children to take home for more practice.

Write the words.

ant   animal   ask   all

Write the sentence.

All my friends play ball.

On Your Own   Write words to finish the sentence.

I can play

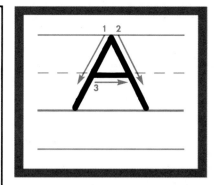

Touch the headline; **slant left** to the baseline. Lift. Touch the headline; **slant right** to the baseline. Lift. Touch the midline; **slide right**.

Shape

Circle your best letter that has a / line.

43

Fun and Games

auditory	visual	kinesthetic

 **Apply**

Before the children write the words and sentence on the page, write *ant* three ways: with letters correctly shaped, shaped too wide, and shaped too narrow. Have them comment on the shape of the letters in each word. Observe the children as they complete the page and respond to **On Your Own**.

Shape

Help the children evaluate the shape of the letters they wrote by comparing them with the models. Then have them respond to the directions in the Key feature at the bottom of the page.

PRACTICE MASTERS 31–32

Name:

Write the letter and the words.

a a a a a a a a a

aid   also   air   apple

at   as   ago   about

Copyright © Zaner-Bloser, Inc.   Practice Master 31

Amy saw the Andes.

Practice Master 32   Copyright © Zaner-Bloser, Inc.

Coaching Hint

Writing Lines Children vary in their ability to write within the confines of a designated area. Some children may need to use paper with wider writing spaces. The teacher should decide what type of paper is best for individuals.

Listen and Write Record letter names and stroke descriptions on an audiocassette tape. Use these letters: **A, a, O, o, T, t, I, i, L, l.** Provide a cassette player. Invite children to listen and write the letters, following the descriptions on the tape.

Phonics Connection

Prepare a tray of wet sand or shaving cream on a table. Tell children to listen for words that begin with the first sound they hear in *alligator*. Then say words such as *ask, apple, dog, tree,* and *ax*. Tell children to write **a** in the sand or shaving cream if the word begins like *alligator*. Repeat with names of people, and have children write **A**.

T43

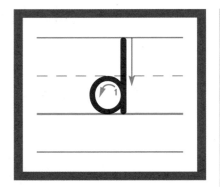

Touch below the midline; **circle back** (left) all the way around. **Push up straight** to the headline. **Pull down straight** to the baseline.

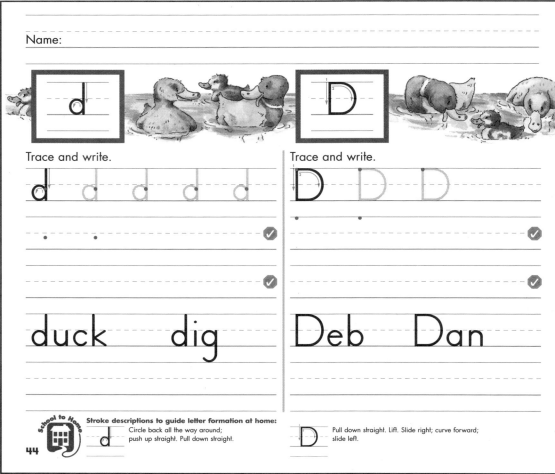

Name:

Trace and write.

d d d d d

duck   dig

Trace and write.

D D D

Deb   Dan

School to Home

Stroke descriptions to guide letter formation at home:
Circle back all the way around; push up straight. Pull down straight.

Pull down straight. Lift. Slide right; curve forward; slide left.

44

---

1. Present the Letter

Have the children look at the model of lowercase **d**. Help them see that after the complete circle, they push up straight to the headline and then pull down straight to the baseline.

Model Write **d** on guidelines as you say the stroke description. Have the children use their index finger to trace the model **d** in their books as you repeat the description.

Practice Let the children practice writing **d** on marker boards or slates or on other paper before they write on the pages.

2. Write and Evaluate

Ask children to trace the shaded letters with pencil, beginning each one at the dot. Then have them write two rows of letters and the words with **d**.

Stop and Check This icon directs the children to stop and circle their best letter.

To help them evaluate **d,** ask:
• Is your circle round?
• Does your **d** touch the headline?

*Repeat teaching steps 1 and 2 for uppercase **D**.*

To help children evaluate **D**, ask:
• Does your **D** curve at the right place?
• Are your slide right and slide left strokes about the same width?

Corrective Strategy

To help the children make the pull down straight stroke touch the right side of the circle, place three dots as shown. Color the middle dot to show where the backward circle begins and ends. As the children write **d,** say the stroke description and refer to the dots.

School to Home

Families may use the stroke descriptions on the student page to encourage good letter formation at home. Copy and distribute **Practice Master 89** for children to take home for more practice.

Write the words.

dad   doll   dive   do

Write the sentence.

Do you like dinosaurs?

On Your Own Write words to finish the sentence.

Dinosaurs are

Shape
Circle your best letter that has a ◯ line.

45

Touch the headline; **pull down straight** to the baseline. Lift. Touch the headline; **slide right; curve forward** (right) to the baseline; **slide left**.

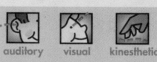

Fun and Games

Letter Walk Use sidewalk chalk to write on the playground several giant-size manuscript letters the children have been learning. Invite children to walk, hop, or skip along the lines of the letters. Ask them to point out the four kinds of lines that make up manuscript letters: horizontal, vertical, circle, and slant.

Clay Letters Invite children to make **d** and **D** from modeling clay. Then have them work in pairs, one saying the stroke descriptions and the other tracing the clay letters, first with eyes open and then closed. Have children reverse roles. They may want to make other letters or write their names with the clay.

Apply

Before the children write the words and sentence on the page, call attention to the shape of the letters. Have them name and trace letters made with only straight lines, only a backward circle, and a combination of both. Observe the children as they complete the page and respond to **On Your Own**.

Shape

Help the children evaluate the shape of the letters they wrote by comparing them with the models. Then have them respond to the direction in the Key feature at the bottom of the page.

PRACTICE MASTERS 33–34

Name:

Write the letter and the words.

d d d d d d d

dial   day   deal   dirt

dear   did   draw   dog

Copyright © Zaner-Bloser, Inc.   Practice Master 33

Dottie danced in Denver.

Practice Master 34   Copyright © Zaner-Bloser, Inc.

Coaching Hint

Basic Strokes To help children develop familiarity with slide right and slide left strokes, have them stand along a line of masking tape on the floor with their feet together facing you. Demonstrate how to slide right and slide left along the line. Have the children demonstrate each slide as you name it. (auditory, kinesthetic)

Practice and Application

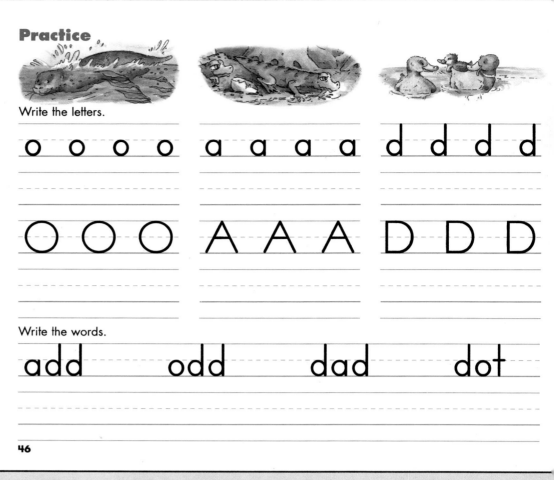

Practice

Write the letters.

o o o o   a a a a   d d d d

O O O   A A A   D D D

Write the words.

add   odd   dad   dot

46

1. Review the Letters

Direct the children to look at the letters being reviewed on student page 46. Ask them what they remember about the shape of most of these letters. *(All but A are made with circle or curve lines.)*

Review the stroke descriptions and model again any of the letters the children may be having difficulty writing.

Ask a volunteer to give a verbal description of one of these letters: **o, a, d, O, A, D**. Challenge the other children to identify the letter being described and then write it on guidelines on the chalkboard.

2. Write and Evaluate

Tell the children to write the letters, beginning each one at the proper starting point. Then have them write the words on the page. Remind the children to form their letters with correct shape so they will be easy to read.

✓ Stop and Check

To help children evaluate their lowercase letters, ask:

- Does your **o** begin just below the midline?
- Does your **a** rest on the baseline?
- Does your **d** touch both the headline and the baseline?

To help children evaluate their uppercase letters, ask:

- Is your **O** round?
- Are your slant strokes in **A** straight?
- Is your **D** about the same width as the model?

Corrective Strategy

To help the children write **d**, remind them to begin the backward circle below the midline.

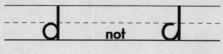

d   not   d

More About Practice

Handwriting practice is most beneficial when it is done in the child's primary modality. Kinesthetic learners will enjoy forming letters with blocks or writing large letters on the chalkboard. Auditory learners may write letters as they listen to a recording of the stroke descriptions. Visual learners will benefit from writing directly under a model you have prepared.

Application Write the naming words.

dog

toad

Dan

apple

yard

Amy

My Words

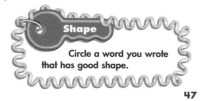

Shape

Circle a word you wrote
that has good shape.

47

Write Away

My Yard Ask children what they think about when they hear the word *yard*. Write their ideas on sentence strips. Let each child select one word to illustrate and write, by itself or in a sentence, using the sentence-strip model. Encourage children to write their own stories about yards.

3 Apply

Before children write the naming words on student page 47, ask volunteers to look at the page and identify strokes they recognize in the letters. Remind children to write their letters with proper shape so they will be easy to read. Observe children as they write on the page.

My Words Ask children to write naming words of their own. Encourage them to write words that contain the review letters. If they need help, suggest they look for words on the previous pages.

Shape

Help children summarize what they have learned about shape. Then have them respond to the direction in the Key feature.

Special Helps

To increase the child's ability to hold the writing implement easily and use it to write accurate, controlled strokes, try this activity. Have the child follow your demonstration of moving or "inchworming" a small object, such as a bottle cap, a coin, or a small toy, from within the closed fist to holding it between the thumb and forefinger of the writing hand. This should be done without assistance from the non-writing hand.

When the child performs this task easily, have him or her reverse the motion, moving the object from the thumb and forefinger back into the closed fist.

—*Maureen King, O.T.R.*

Fun and Games

auditory   visual   kinesthetic

What's in the Basket? Draw the outline of a large laundry or utility basket on the chalkboard and add guidelines. Give clues to identify something commonly found in a yard, and ask a child to name it and to write it on the basket. Classmates can help with spelling. After the child writes, ask a volunteer to name the kinds of strokes in the letters. Invite another volunteer to tell where each letter begins and ends. Erase the word and start again.

Touch below the headline; **curve forward** (right) to the midline; **pull down straight** to halfway between the midline and the baseline. Lift. Dot.

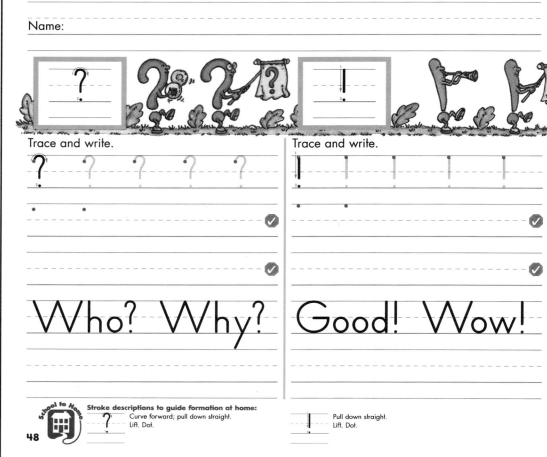

Name:

Trace and write.

? ? ? ? ?

Who? Why?

Trace and write.

Good! Wow!

Stroke descriptions to guide formation at home:

? Curve forward; pull down straight. Lift. Dot.

| Pull down straight. Lift. Dot.

48

---

1. Present the Marks

Direct children to look at the model of the question mark on student page 48. Ask them to tell what it looks like (*a hook with a dot under it*).

Model Write ? on guidelines as you say the stroke description. Model writing ? in the air as you repeat the stroke description. Have children echo it as they write ? in the air with you.

Practice Let the children practice writing ? on marker boards or slates or on other paper before they write on the pages.

2. Write and Evaluate

Ask children to trace the shaded question marks with pencil, beginning each one at the starting dot. Then ask children to write question marks and the words followed by punctuation marks.

✓ **Stop and Check** This icon directs children to stop and circle their best punctuation mark.

To help them evaluate ?, ask:

- Is your question mark about the same width as the model?
- Does it begin with a curve forward and end with a pull down straight stroke?
- Does it have a dot on the baseline?

Repeat teaching steps 1 and 2 for the exclamation point.

To help children evaluate !, ask:

- Does your exclamation point begin at the headline?
- Is it vertical?
- Does your dot rest on the baseline directly under the vertical stroke?

Corrective Strategy

To help children write ? the correct width, place a green dot for *start* and a red dot for the end of the curve. Have children make the curve. Show them how to make a pull down straight stroke, lift, and add a dot correctly aligned.

Write the sentences.

Can you come over?

I will see you soon!

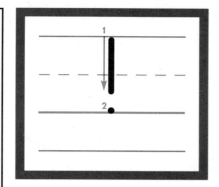

Touch the headline; **pull down straight** to halfway between the midline and the baseline. Lift. Dot.

 Write words to finish the sentence.

I like to see

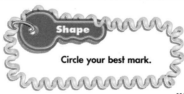
Circle your best mark.

49

 Apply

Before the children write the sentences and the ending marks, call attention to the space between the last letter in the word and the question mark or exclamation point. Point out that this is about the same amount of space as between letters. Observe the children as they complete the page and respond to **On Your Own**.

Shape

Help the children evaluate the shape of the letters and punctuation marks they wrote by comparing them with the models. Guide them to recognize why one punctuation mark might be better than another. Then have them respond to the direction in the Key feature at the bottom of the page.

Coaching Hint

Touch and Trace Make **?** and **!** from beans or sandpaper. Children who are having difficulty forming these punctuation marks can trace the tactile versions several times with their fingers and then practice writing each end mark on the chalkboard. (kinesthetic)

Fun and Games

auditory   visual   kinesthetic

Mobiles: ! and ? Draw exclamation points and question marks on card stock or construction paper. Ask the children to cut these out and add designs. Attach the dots. Then have them write either a question or an exclamation on an index card with guidelines. Attach the card to the correct punctuation mark, and hang the punctuation mobiles. Invite children to share their exclamations and questions with classmates.

Featured Letters

cC eE fF
gG jJ qQ

Featured Key to Legibility:

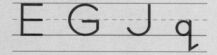
Size

Size refers to the relationship in height of the letters to each other and to the writing space. By writing on consistently spaced guidelines, children learn to make their letters in correct proportion to one another.

Other Acceptable Letterforms

The following letterforms are acceptable variations of the models shown in this book.

E G J q

Alternate Letter Formation

Use these stroke descriptions to show an alternate method for children who have difficulty using the continuous-stroke method.

g **Circle back** all the way around. Lift. **Pull down straight; curve back.**

q **Circle back** all the way around. Lift. **Pull down straight; curve forward.**

Keys to Legibility
Make your writing easy to read. Look at the size of each letter.

Size

These letters are just the right size.

Writing is fun!

This writing is easy to read.

Tall Letters
Tall letters touch the headline.

K b d

Short Letters
Short letters touch the midline.

o m e

Letters That Go Below the Baseline
Some letters go below the baseline.

j g y

50

1. Present the Key

Point out the Key feature at the top of student page 50. Explain to children that they will see this feature often in the coming pages. It directs them to consider the size of each letter they write. Ask children to tell what they notice about the letters in the sentence on the student page. Help them notice the use of guidelines to make all the letters consistent in size. Point out that letters of consistent size are easier to read.

Direct the children to look at the animals on the page. Point out that the kangaroo is showing that letters may be tall, touching both the headline and the baseline. The owl shows short letters that touch the midline and the baseline. The jaguar shows that some letters go below the baseline and touch the next headline.

2. Trace and Evaluate

Write letters from the page on guidelines on the chalkboard. Have volunteers come to the board and use chalk of different colors to trace a letter in a group that you name. Guide children in evaluating the quality of consistent size in the letters, noticing how the letters fit between the headline and the baseline, the midline and the baseline, or the midline and the headline of the next writing space.

Read the directions for the first row of letters on student page 51. Encourage the children to trace and write the tall letters. Have them continue in the same way, tracing and then writing the short letters and the letters that go below the baseline.

Trace and write tall letters.

T O A L D t d

Trace and write short letters.

a o c i e v r n

Trace and write letters that go below the baseline.

g p j q y

51

Teaching the Letters: Modeling

Modeling is a *think aloud* process in which a teacher verbalizes his or her thinking. The stroke descriptions aid the modeling process. For example, in modeling the letter **j,** the teacher might say, "As I write the letter **j,** I start at the broken midline. Then I pull down straight through the red baseline toward the headline of the next writing space and then curve back. Am I finished? No, I have to dot the **j** about halfway between the headline and the midline."

Support Materials

These support products and materials for the beginning writer are available in the **Handwriting** section of the Zaner-Bloser catalog.

- *Now I Know My ABCs* (a multimodal kit-in-a-book)
- *Now I Know My 1,2,3's* (a multimodal kit-in-a-book)
- *Touch and Trace Letter Cards*
- *Read, Write, and Color Alphabet Mat*
- *Manuscript Alphabet Wall Strips*
- *Illustrated Manuscript Alphabet Strips*
- *Self-Adhesive Manuscript Alphabet Desk Strips*
- *Writing Journals* and *Story Journals*

Meeting Individual Needs

for auditory learners
Explain that tall letters could be like adults, short letters like children, and letters that go below the baseline like pets with tails. Name several letters and ask volunteers to tell whether each letter is like an adult, a child, or a pet.

for visual learners
Give children writing paper. Have them write each letter in the lesson several times with different-colored crayons.

for kinesthetic learners
Provide Zaner-Bloser *Touch and Trace Letter Cards* or letters cut from sandpaper. Have the children quietly say the strokes as they trace the letters three times.

What the research says . . .

Many educators believe that handwriting instruction should begin at the chalkboard where children have plenty of space, can use large muscles, and can make corrections easily.

—Elinor P. Ross and Betty D. Roe, *Handwriting Instruction.* © Wadsworth

Note: The chalkboard permits easy integration of handwriting instruction with other content areas and with day-to-day communication in the classroom.

T51

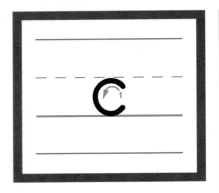

Touch below the midline; **circle back** (left), ending above the baseline.

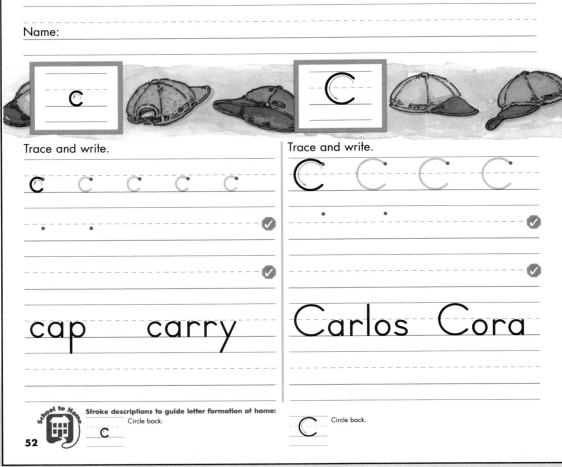

Name:

Trace and write.

c c c c c

cap   carry

Trace and write.

C C C C

Carlos Cora

Stroke descriptions to guide letter formation at home:
Circle back.

c

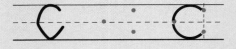
Circle back.

---

1. Present the Letter

Direct the children to look at lowercase **c**. Help them recognize that the letter begins and ends at points between the midline and the baseline.

Model Write **c** on guidelines as you say the stroke descriptions. Model writing **c** in the air as you repeat the description. Have the children say the strokes as they write **c** in the air with you.

Practice Let the children practice writing **c** on marker boards or slates or on other paper before they write on the pages.

2. Write and Evaluate

Ask the children to trace the shaded letters with pencil, beginning each one at the dot. Then have them write two rows of letters and the words with **c**.

Stop and Check This icon directs the children to stop and circle their best letter.

To help them evaluate **c,** ask:

- Does your **c** look like a circle that has not been closed?
- Does your **c** stop a little above the baseline?

*Repeat teaching steps 1 and 2 for uppercase **C**.*

To help children evaluate **C,** ask:

- Is your **C** about the same width as the model?
- Does your **C** rest on the baseline?

Corrective Strategy

To help children begin and end **C** correctly, make three dots representing the beginning, middle, and end of the letter. Invite them to write the letter using the dots as a guide. Check alignment by drawing a vertical line between beginning and end dots.

C   C

Families may use the stroke descriptions on the student page to encourage good letter formation at home. Copy and distribute **Practice Master 90** for children to take home for more practice.

Write the words.

coat   car   cook   cut

Write the sentence.

Can you count to 20?

On Your Own Write words that begin with **c** or **C**.

Size

Circle your best short letter.

53

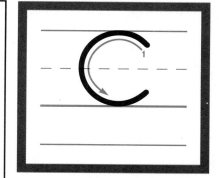

Touch below the headline;
circle back (left), ending
above the baseline.

Apply

Before the children write the words and sentence, ask them to look at the page and identify letters that are tall or short and that have a descender. Remind them of the importance of using the guidelines so their letters will be the correct size. Observe the children as they complete the page and respond to **On Your Own**.

Size

Help the children evaluate the size of the letters they wrote by comparing them with the models. Then have them respond to the direction in the Key feature at the bottom of the page.

PRACTICE MASTERS 35–36

Name:

Write the letter and the words.

c   c   c   c   c   c   c   c

cloud   call   curl   close

cave   city   can   circus

Copyright © Zaner-Bloser, Inc.   Practice Master 35

Chase called me in China.

Practice Master 36   Copyright © Zaner-Bloser, Inc.

Coaching Hint

Basic Strokes To help children with the backward circle, make a large circle on the floor with tape. Ask the children to walk, hop, or jump around the circle in a counter-clockwise direction. (kinesthetic)

Fun and Games

auditory   visual   kinesthetic

Letter Pictures On the chalkboard, model how to draw a cat using only **c**'s. Ask the children what other animals' names begin with the same **c** sound they hear in *cat*, such as *caterpillar* and *cougar*. Invite them to draw their own animal, using **c**'s, and label it.

Cookie Jar Have each child write **Cc** on a brown paper circle (cookie). Invite children to think of words that begin with **c** as in *cookie*. When a child names a word, he or she can place the cookie on a bulletin board cookie jar.

T53

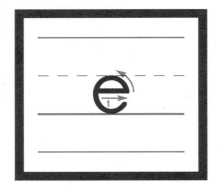

Touch halfway between the midline and baseline; **slide right; circle back** (left), ending above the baseline.

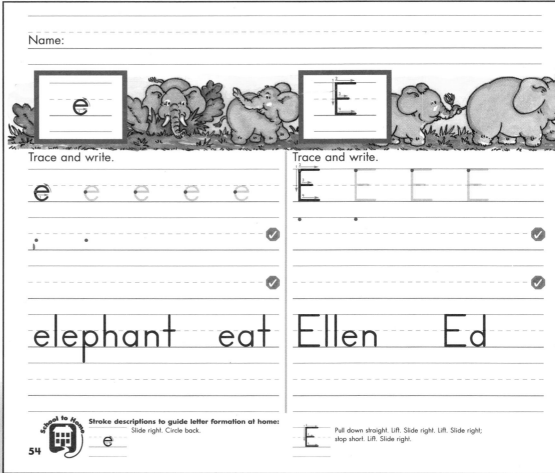

Name:

Trace and write.

e e e e e

elephant eat

Trace and write.

E E E E

Ellen Ed

Stroke descriptions to guide letter formation at home:
Slide right. Circle back.

e

Pull down straight. Lift. Slide right. Lift. Slide right; stop short. Lift. Slide right.

E

---

1. Present the Letter

Direct the children to look at lowercase **e**. Make sure they see that the slide right stroke is between the midline and the baseline.

Model Write **e** on guidelines as you say the stroke description. Invite the children to use their index finger to write **e**'s on their desktop as you give the description and they repeat it.

Practice Let the children practice writing **e** on marker boards or slates or on other paper before they write on the pages.

2. Write and Evaluate

Ask the children to trace the shaded letters with pencil, beginning each one at the dot. Then ask them to write two rows of letters and the words with **e**.

Stop and Check This icon directs the children to stop and circle their best letter.

To help them evaluate **e,** ask:
• Does your **e** look round?
• Is your slide right stroke straight?

Repeat teaching steps 1 and 2 for uppercase E.

To help children evaluate **E,** ask:
• Are your top and bottom slide right strokes the same width?
• Is your **E** about the same width as the model?

Corrective Strategy

To help the children touch the slide right stroke of **e** when circling back, place a dot where the slide right starts and a dot where it ends. Demonstrate how to connect the dots and then circle back, remembering to touch the beginning dot.

Families may use the stroke descriptions on the student page to encourage good letter formation at home. Copy and distribute **Practice Master 91** for children to take home for more practice.

Write the words.

egg   end   empty   exit

Write the sentence.

Everyone enjoys stories.

 On Your Own Write words that have **e** or **E** in them.

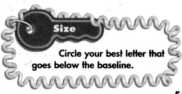
Size
Circle your best letter that goes below the baseline.

55

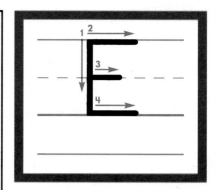

Touch the headline; **pull down straight** to the baseline. Lift. Touch the headline; **slide right**. Lift. Touch the midline; **slide right**. Stop short. Lift. Touch the baseline; **slide right**.

Fun and Games

auditory   visual   kinesthetic

Apply

Before the children write the words and sentence on the page, remind them that all uppercase letters are tall and touch both the headline and the baseline. None of them go below the baseline, as some lowercase letters with descenders do. Observe the children as they complete the page and respond to **On Your Own**. After they write, have them compare their letters with the models.

Size

Help the children evaluate the size of the letters they wrote by comparing them with the models. Then have them respond to the direction in the Key feature at the bottom of the page.

PRACTICE MASTERS 37–38

Name:
Write the letter and the words.

e e e e e e e e

ear   else   elm   each

eel   seed   ever   eye

Copyright © Zaner-Bloser, Inc.   Practice Master 37

Elsa left Egypt.

Practice Master 38   Copyright © Zaner-Bloser, Inc.

Coaching Hint

Writing Lines To help children practice using the term *halfway* and locating the position, use masking tape to make two parallel lines on the floor. Have children take turns jumping to the halfway point between the lines. (visual, kinesthetic)

Write With Water Place cups of water near the chalkboard. Invite children to practice writing letters and words by dipping their finger or paintbrush into the water and writing on the chalkboard. Help children form mental images of the letters by watching as the letters disappear.

Phonics Connection
Write word groups such as these on guidelines on the chalkboard: *bed, red, fed; net, pet, set; ten, hen, men; see, bee, tree*. Read each group with the children. Then ask questions such as "Which word names something to sleep on?" Have a child point to the word that answers the question and trace over the **e** with colored chalk.

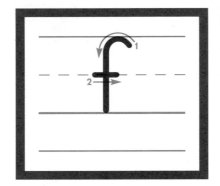

Touch below the headline; **curve back** (left); **pull down straight** to the baseline. Lift. Touch the midline; **slide right**.

Name:

Trace and write.

f f f f

fish   find

Trace and write.

F F F F

Fred   Flora

School to Home

Stroke descriptions to guide letter formation at home:

f — Curve back; pull down straight. Lift. Slide right.

F — Pull down straight. Lift. Slide right. Lift. Slide right; stop short.

56

1. Present the Letter

Have the children look at the model of lowercase **f**. Point out that **f** is a tall letter, touching both the headline and the baseline.

Model Write **f** on guidelines as you say the stroke description. Model writing **f** in the air as you repeat the description. Have the children say the names of the strokes as they write **f** in the air with you.

Practice Let the children practice writing **f** on marker boards or slates or on other paper before they write on the pages.

2. Write and Evaluate

Ask the children to trace the shaded letters with pencil, beginning each one at the dot. Then ask them to write two rows of letters and the words with **f**.

 Stop and Check This icon directs the children to stop and circle their best letter.

To help them evaluate **f**, ask:
- Does your **f** rest on the baseline?
- Is your slide right on the midline?

Repeat teaching steps 1 and 2 for uppercase F.

To help children evaluate **F**, ask:
- Is your letter straight up and down?
- Does your second slide right line stop short?

Corrective Strategy

To help the children write the slide right strokes of **F** the correct width, have them first write the pull down straight stroke. Place dots to indicate where the slide right strokes should end. Have them complete **F** as you say the stroke description.

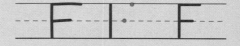

School to Home

Families may use the stroke descriptions on the student page to encourage good letter formation at home. Copy and distribute **Practice Master 92** for children to take home for more practice.

Write the words.

fun   family   fall   fly

Write the sentence.

Friends have lots of fun.

On Your Own Write number words that begin with **f** or **F**.

Circle your best tall letter.

57

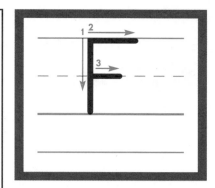

Touch the headline; **pull down straight** to the baseline. Lift. Touch the headline; **slide right**. Lift. Touch the midline; **slide right**. Stop short.

Fun and Games

auditory   visual   kinesthetic

Tongue Twisters Say this **F** tongue twister for the children. Then have them say it slowly, then quickly, with you: *Fran fed Fred's frog.* Explain that in a tongue twister, the same sound is repeated in most words. Have children make up their own **F** tongue twisters. Then have them write **f** or **F** on lined paper. Say the tongue twisters, and have children point to **f** or **F** each time they hear /**f**/.

Fish Fun Cover a bulletin board with blue paper. Have children sponge paint different colors on drawing paper. When the paper is dry, help them draw and cut out large fish shapes. Have the children label the fish with **f** and **F**. Place the fish on the blue paper to create a sea scene.

Apply

Before the children write the words and sentence on the page, have them share what they know about using the guidelines to make their letters the correct size. Observe the children as they complete the page and respond to **On Your Own**.

Size

Help the children evaluate the size of the letters they wrote by comparing them with the models. Then have them respond to the direction in the Key feature at the bottom of the page.

PRACTICE MASTERS 39–40

Name:

Write the letter and the words.

f f f f f f f f

fold   feet   farm   fill

feel   for   foot   fire

Copyright © Zaner-Bloser, Inc.   Practice Master 39

Frank flew to France.

Practice Master 40   Copyright © Zaner-Bloser, Inc.

Coaching Hint

Pencil Position Holding a pencil too tightly causes children to tire easily when writing. Have them crumple a piece of paper and hold it in the palm of the hand and then pick up the pencil. This will help them avoid squeezing the pencil. (kinesthetic)

T57

Practice and Application

Write the letters.

c c c c   e e e e   f f f f

C C C   E E E   F F F

Write the words.

face   feet   ice   life

58

1. Review the Letters

Direct the children to look at the letters being reviewed on student page 58. Ask them what they remember about the size of these letters. (*c and e are short; f, C, E, and F are tall; all fit on the guidelines*)

Review the stroke descriptions and model again any of the letters the children may be having difficulty writing.

Ask a volunteer to give a verbal description of one of these letters: **c, e, f, C, E, F**. Challenge the other children to identify the letter being described and then write it on guidelines on the chalkboard.

2. Write and Evaluate

Tell the children to write the letters, beginning each one at the proper starting point. Then have them write the words on the page. Remind children to use the guidelines to help them form letters with correct size.

Stop and Check

To help children evaluate their lowercase letters, ask:

- Does your **c** begin just below the midline?
- Is the slide right stroke in your **e** straight?
- Is your **f** crossed on the midline?

To help children evaluate their uppercase letters, ask:

- Is your **C** round?
- Does your **E** touch both the headline and the baseline?
- Is your **F** straight up and down?

Corrective Strategy

To help the children write **E**, remind them to write their slide right strokes on the appropriate guidelines.

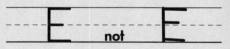

More About Practice

Children learning to write need a variety of meaningful ways to use their new skills. Ask children to practice handwriting as they fill in classroom forms, make lists of favorite things, write cards and notes to classmates, and label pictures they draw. Encourage children to evaluate their handwriting across the curriculum—not just during "handwriting time."

eat

fill

catch

feed

call

color

My Words

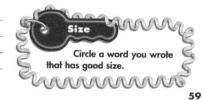

Size

Circle a word you wrote that has good size.

59

Write Away

Action Words Review the action words on the student page. Encourage discussion about other kinds of action a person can carry out and write the words on guidelines on the chalkboard. Have children choose one of the words and write a phrase or a sentence about someone they know or about themselves doing the action.

3 Apply

Before children write the action words on student page 59, ask volunteers to look at the page and tell what they notice about the size of the letters. Remind children to use the guidelines as they write so their letters will be the correct size. Observe children as they write on the page.

My Words Ask children to write action words of their own. Encourage them to write words that contain the review letters. If they need help, suggest they look for words on the previous pages.

Size

Help children summarize what they have learned about size. Then have them respond to the direction in the Key feature.

Special Helps

To assist the child who is still switching his or her preferred writing hand, try this activity. Provide a vertical game such as Connect Four. Center the game pieces in front of the child. Have the child place pieces into the top of the game board, using the hand of his or her choice. The non-preferred hand should be used to hold and steady the game board. The child can switch hands and repeat the task to experience which felt better.

—Maureen King, O.T.R.

Fun and Games

auditory   visual   kinesthetic

Lights! Camera! Action! Select a child to choose one of the action words on the student page and to pantomime it for the class to guess. After all the words have been guessed correctly, have more volunteers act out other action words. When a classmate guesses the word, you or one of the children should write the new action word on guidelines on the chalkboard.

Touch below the midline; **circle back** (left) all the way around. **Push up straight** to the midline. **Pull down straight** through the baseline; **curve back** (left).

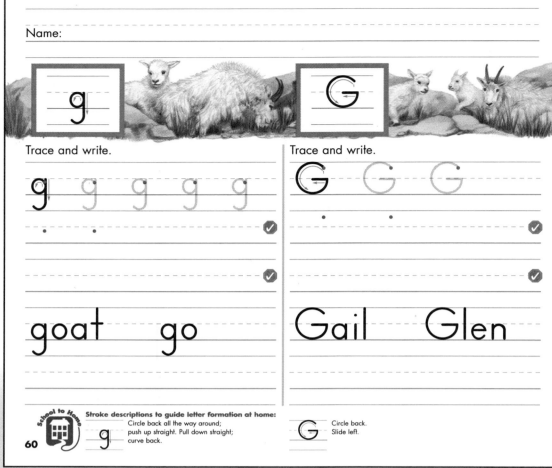

Name:

Trace and write.

g g g g g

✓

✓

goat   go

Trace and write.

G G G

✓

✓

Gail   Glen

School to Home

Stroke descriptions to guide letter formation at home:

g — Circle back all the way around; push up straight. Pull down straight; curve back.

G — Circle back. Slide left.

60

① Present the Letter

Direct the children to look at lowercase **g**. Focus attention on the letter's shape by pointing out how part of the letter goes below the baseline.

Model Write **g** on guidelines as you say the stroke description. Invite several children to dip a small sponge in water and use it to write **g** on the chalkboard while others say the description with you.

Practice Let the children practice writing **g** on marker boards or slates or on other paper before they write on the page.

② Write and Evaluate

Ask the children to trace the shaded letters with pencil, beginning each one at the dot. Then ask them to write two rows of letters and the words with **g**.

✓ Stop and Check This icon directs the children to stop and circle their best letter.

To help them evaluate **g**, ask:
• Is your **g** straight up and down?
• Does your **g** end below the baseline?

*Repeat teaching steps 1 and 2 for uppercase **G**.*

To help children evaluate **G**, ask:
• Is your slide left on the midline?
• Is your **G** about the same width as the model?

Corrective Strategy

To help the children start and end the slide left stroke of **G** correctly, dot around a backward circle and place two **x**'s on the midline as shown. Demonstrate how to stop before making the slide left stroke on the midline. Have children trace your **G**.

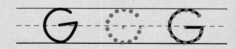

School to Home

Families may use the stroke descriptions on the student page to encourage good letter formation at home. Copy and distribute **Practice Master 93** for children to take home for more practice.

T60

Write the words.

girl   gate   goes   got

Write the sentence.

Get ready, get set, giggle!

On Your Own Write words that begin with **g** or **G**.

Size
Circle your best letter
that goes below the baseline.

61

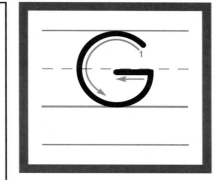

Touch below the headline;
circle back (left), ending at
the midline. **Slide left**.

Fun and Games

auditory   visual   kinesthetic

Frame It Make a picture frame out of tagboard. Hang the frame around a target letter on a prepared alphabet wall chart or around a letter-form you write on the chalkboard. As children find the featured letter in their writing, they should draw a frame around it. At the end of the day, ask children to look at all the letterforms they framed. Ask, "Do you notice improvement in your writing?"

Shape and Trace In a shoebox, place pieces of yarn or string, pipe cleaners, craft sticks, paper strips and circles, and cotton swabs. Invite children to work in pairs. Have them use the materials to form **g** and **G**. Then have partners take turns saying descriptions and tracing the letters.

Apply

Before the children write the words and sentence on the page, write words from the sentence on guidelines on the chalkboard. Make some obvious errors in the size of some of the letters. Encourage the children to help you correct your errors. Then observe the children as they complete the page and respond to **On Your Own**.

Size

Help the children evaluate the size of the letters they wrote by comparing them with the models. Then have them respond to the direction in the Key feature at the bottom of the page.

PRACTICE MASTERS 41–42

Name:

Write the letter and the words.

g g g g g g g g

gold   glass   goal   get

good   green   grass   game

Copyright © Zaner-Bloser, Inc.   Practice Master 41

Gia goes to Greece.

Practice Master 42   Copyright © Zaner-Bloser, Inc.

Coaching Hint

Paper Position To assure that the paper is placed correctly, for both right- and left-handed children, use tape to form a frame on the desk so the children will be able to place the paper in the correct position. (visual)

T61

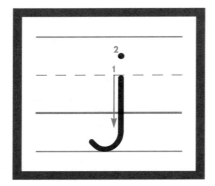

Touch the midline; **pull down straight** through the baseline; **curve back** (left). Lift. **Dot.**

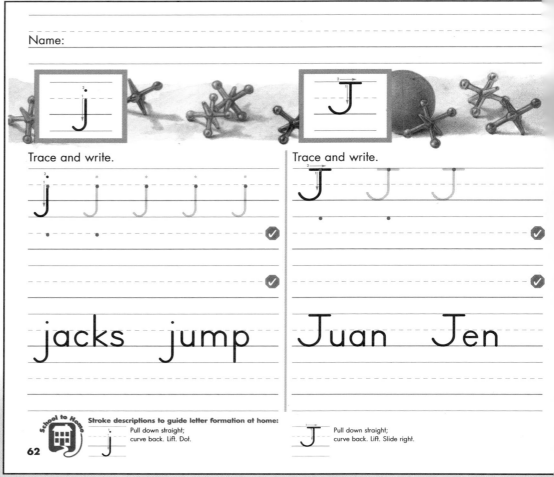

Name: _____

Trace and write.

j j j j j

jacks jump

Trace and write.

J J J

Juan Jen

Stroke descriptions to guide letter formation at home:

Pull down straight; curve back. Lift. Dot.

Pull down straight; curve back. Lift. Slide right.

---

1. Present the Letter

Direct the children to look at lowercase **j**. Help the children recognize that **j** and **g** have the same ending. Ask if they know a letter that has a **j** in it without the dot. (*g*)

Model Write **j** on guidelines as you say the stroke description. Invite children to use an index finger to write **j** on their desktop. Have them say the description with you as they write.

Practice Let the children practice writing **j** on marker boards or slates or on other paper before they write on the pages.

2. Write and Evaluate

Ask the children to trace the shaded letters with pencil, beginning each one at the dot. Then ask them to write two rows of letters and the words with **j**.

Stop and Check This icon directs the children to stop and circle their best letter.

To help them evaluate **j**, ask:
• Is the bottom of your **j** round?
• Is your dot about halfway between the headline and midline?

*Repeat teaching steps 1 and 2 for uppercase **J**.*

To help children evaluate **J**, ask:
• Does your **J** begin at the headline?
• Is the bottom round?

Corrective Strategy

To help the children begin the curve of **j** in the right place, demonstrate how to make the curve, starting between the baseline and the next writing line. Mark this spot with a dot as the children write **j**, turning from a straight line into a curve.

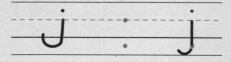

Families may use the stroke descriptions on the student page to encourage good letter formation at home. Copy and distribute **Practice Master 94** for children to take home for more practice.

Write the words.

jam   jar   joke   jog

Write the sentence.

Join our jumping game.

Touch the headline; **pull down straight; curve back** (left). Lift. Touch the headline; **slide right**.

On Your Own Write words that begin with **j** or **J**.

Circle your best short letter.

63

Apply

Before the children write the words and sentence on the page, have them compare the formation of the letters **g** and **j** in the word *jog*. Note similarities in size, shape, and placement. Observe the children as they complete the page and respond to **On Your Own**. After they write, have them compare their **g** and **j** with the models. Guide them to recognize why one letter might be better than another.

Size

Help the children evaluate the size of the letters they wrote by comparing them with the models. Then have them respond to the direction in the Key feature at the bottom of the page.

PRACTICE MASTERS 43–44

Name:

Write the letter and the words.

j j j j j j j j

jay   joy   just   juice

jug   jet   junk   job

Copyright © Zaner-Bloser, Inc.   Practice Master 43

Julio jets in July.

Practice Master 44   Copyright © Zaner-Bloser, Inc.

Coaching Hint

Shape Call attention to the part of a letter that descends below the baseline by writing **g** and **j** on guidelines on the chalkboard. Have children trace the descending strokes with colored chalk to highlight their shape. (visual, kinesthetic)

Fun and Games

 auditory   visual   kinesthetic

Letter Jump Use masking tape to form giant-size **j** and **J** on the classroom floor. Invite children to jump along the outline of one of the letters as you say directions for forming it. Then have children hop, walk, or tiptoe along the letters.

Phonics Connection Write guidelines on the chalkboard. After everyone agrees that *jump* begins with **j,** ask the children to jump up every time they hear a word that begins like *jump.* Say a series of words, several of which begin with **j**. Have a child write **j** on the chalkboard if the word begins with **j**.

T63

Touch below the midline; **circle back** (left) all the way around. **Push up straight** to the midline. **Pull down straight** through the baseline; **curve forward** (right).

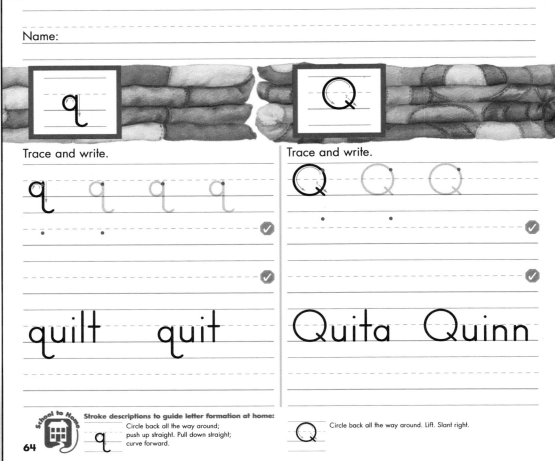

Name:

Trace and write.

q q q q

quilt   quit

Trace and write.

Q Q Q

Quita Quinn

Stroke descriptions to guide letter formation at home:

q Circle back all the way around; push up straight. Pull down straight; curve forward.

Q Circle back all the way around. Lift. Slant right.

Present the Letter

Have the children look at lowercase **q**. Focus attention on the letter's shape by helping the children recognize how **q** is just like **g** except for the direction of the ending stroke. Point to the letters **o** and **a** in **q**.

Model Write **q** on guidelines as you say the stroke description. Model using your finger to write **q** on sandpaper or on the **q** card from Zaner-Bloser's *Touch and Trace Letter Cards*. Pair children and have them take turns following your model and saying the stroke description.

Practice Let the children practice writing **q** on marker boards or slates or on other paper before they write on the pages.

2. **Write and Evaluate**

Ask the children to trace the shaded letters with pencil, beginning each one at the dot. Then ask them to write two rows of letters and the words with **q**.

Stop and Check This icon directs the children to stop and circle their best letter.

To help them evaluate **q**, ask:
- Does your pull down straight stroke touch the right side of the circle?
- Is your **q** made with a backward circle stroke?

Repeat teaching steps 1 and 2 for uppercase Q.

To help children evaluate **Q**, ask:
- Does your **Q** look just like **O** except for the slant right stroke?
- Did you end your slant right on the baseline?

Corrective Strategy

To reinforce continuous strokes in **q**, write **q** three times, each time highlighting a different stroke with a broken line. Invite the children to trace each letter as you say the stroke description. Point out that the curve forward stroke is the bottom of a circle.

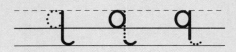

Families may use the stroke descriptions on the student page to encourage good letter formation at home. Copy and distribute **Practice Master 95** for children to take home for more practice.

Write the words.

queen   quart   quarter

Write the sentences.

Quick! It's time to go.

On Your Own Write words that begin with **qu** or **Qu**.

Size
Circle your best tall letter.

65

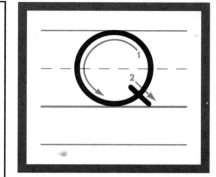

Touch below the headline; **circle back** (left) all the way around. Lift. **Slant right** to the baseline.

Fun and Games

auditory   visual   kinesthetic

Apply

Before the children write the words and sentences on the page, help them identify letters that are short or tall or that have a descender. Observe the children as they complete the page and respond to **On Your Own**.

Size

Help the children evaluate the size of the letters they wrote by comparing them with the models. Then have them respond to the direction in the Key feature at the bottom of the page.

PRACTICE MASTERS 45–46

Name: _____

Write the letter and the words.

q   q   q   q   q   q   q   q

quick   quiz   quack   quite

quill   quail   quote   quest

Copyright © Zaner-Bloser, Inc.   Practice Master 45

Mrs. Quinn called me.

Practice Master 46   Copyright © Zaner-Bloser, Inc.

Coaching Hint

Reversals If children confuse the letters **g** and **q,** provide pipe cleaners so they can make **g** and then follow its shape with their fingers. Ask them to write **g** on their paper three times and circle the best one. Follow the same procedure for **q.** (visual, kinesthetic)

Paint the Letter Make available cotton swabs, several colors of paint, and paper with guidelines. Invite children to write **Q** and **q** with cotton swabs dipped in paint. Have them describe to a partner how they formed each letter. Encourage them to continue by writing words with **q**.

Message Center Designate a section of the chalkboard as a message center. Encourage children to use the message center to write news, questions, jokes and riddles, messages to you, and messages to classmates. Remind children that because their messages are for others to read, they must be legible.

T65

Practice and Application

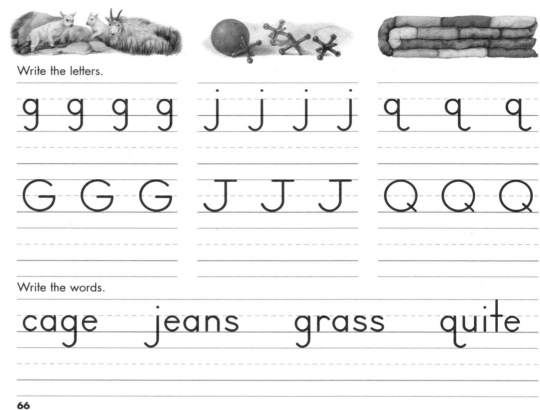

Write the letters.

g g g g j j j j q q q q

G G G J J J Q Q Q

Write the words.

cage   jeans   grass   quite

66

1. Review the Letters

Direct the children to look at the letters being reviewed on student page 66. Ask them what they remember about the size of these letters. (*Some are tall; some are short and go below the baseline.*)

Review the stroke descriptions and model again any of the letters the children may be having difficulty writing.

Ask a volunteer to give a verbal description of one of these letters: **g, j, q, G, J, Q**. Challenge the other children to identify the letter being described and then write it on guidelines on the chalkboard.

2. Write and Evaluate

Direct the children to write the letters, beginning each one at the proper starting point. Then have them write the words on the page. Remind children to form their letters carefully and refer to the models so their letters are easy to read.

✓ Stop and Check

To help children evaluate their lowercase letters, ask:

- Does your **g** go below the baseline and touch the next headline?
- Did you remember to dot your **j**?
- Does your **q** touch the next headline?

To help children evaluate their uppercase letters, ask:

- Does your **G** end with a slide left stroke?
- Is your **J** about the same width as the model?
- Is your **Q** round?

Corrective Strategy

To help the children write **g,** remind them that the descender fills the space below the baseline and touches the next headline.

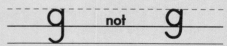

g not g

More About Practice

Add interest to handwriting practice by asking children to write letters in one of these ways: finger-trace on their palms or on a partner's back; write on a MagnaDoodle, magic slate, or similar toy; finger-write in paint or shaving cream; write with markers in a large size on the back of discarded paper; write letters using the drawing tool in a favorite software program.

Application Write the describing words.

juicy

green

good

jolly

quiet

quick

My Words

Size

Circle a word you wrote that has good size.

67

Describing Words Ask children to help you list people, places, or things that can be described. Then have them choose one of the words, write it on their paper, and list as many describing words as they can think of that could describe their chosen word.

Apply

Before children write the describing words on student page 67, ask volunteers to look at the page and identify strokes they recognize in the letters. Remind them to write their letters with proper size so they will be easy to read. Observe children as they write on the page.

My Words Ask children to write describing words of their own. Encourage them to write words that contain the review letters. If they need help, suggest they look for words on the previous pages.

Size

Help children summarize what they have learned about size. Then have them respond to the direction in the Key feature.

Special Helps

The chalkboard is an important tool for handwriting instruction. Children enjoy writing at the board, and the amount of sensory feedback created between chalk and board is an advantage for developing essential fine motor and perceptual skills.

It is important to realize that chalkboards and dry-erase boards do not serve the same functions when it comes to handwriting instruction. For many children, dry-erase markers flow too quickly to aid careful formation of letters. The fluidity of markers can be useful, however, for children who apply too much pencil pressure when they write.

—*Maureen King, O.T.R.*

Fun and Games

 auditory   visual   kinesthetic

Lines and Designs
Distribute drawing paper and crayons. Play some lively music and ask the children to draw as they listen. Then stop the music. Have children share their drawings. As children show their work, ask classmates to identify pictures that were formed with any of the basic strokes: vertical, horizontal, circle, slant.

Featured Letters

uU sS bB pP
rR nN mM hH

Featured Key to Legibility:

Spacing

Spacing between letters, between words, and between sentences must be consistent in writing that is easy to read. Letters should not touch each other or be so far apart that confusion occurs. Evaluating spacing is excellent training for children in visual acuity.

Keys to Legibility

Make your writing easy to read.
Look at the spacing between letters.

Spacing

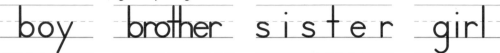

These letters are too close.	These letters are too far apart.	These letters have good spacing.
close	far	good

Circle two words with good spacing between letters.

boy   brother   sister   girl

Trace and write words. Use good spacing between letters.

aunts   uncles   cousins

68

Other Acceptable Letterforms

The following letterforms are acceptable variations of the models shown in this book.

R M

Alternate Letter Formation

Use these stroke descriptions to show an alternate method for children who have difficulty using the continuous-stroke method.

M — **Pull down straight.** Lift. **Slant right.** Lift. **Slant left.** Lift. **Pull down straight.**

1 Present the Key

Point out the Key feature at the top of student page 68. Explain to children that this key directs them to consider the spacing between letters and between words they write.

Direct the children to look at the ducks on the page. Encourage them to describe what they notice. Help them recognize that the spacing between the ducklings is similar to the spacing between the letters in the word boxes. Then help them evaluate the words to determine the two with good spacing.

2 Trace and Evaluate

Read the directions for writing the row of words on student page 68. Encourage the children to trace and then to write carefully, noticing the spacing of the letters in each word.

Read the directions on student page 69 with the children and help them complete the page in their books.

Suggest a simple method children can use anytime to check their spacing: Leave the space of one finger between words and the space of two fingers between sentences. Alternately, provide narrow craft sticks and have the children draw a spaceman face on one end. Left-handed writers may find using this stick more convenient, since their fingers may tend to block the writing.

Make your writing easy to read.
Look at the spacing between words.

These words have good spacing.

This is just right.

There is a finger space between words.

Write a ✔ next to the sentence that has good spacing between words.

This is easy to read.

This is hard to read.

Write the sentence. Use good spacing between words.

I can read this.

69

Teaching the Letters:
Warming Up for Writing

Motivate children to write new letters by having them write a favorite letter first. The warm-up letter may be a first or last initial or a letter the child writes especially well and enjoys writing. Warming up this way will help children begin a piece of writing with success and confidence.

Meeting Individual Needs

for auditory learners
Write **U, S, B, P, R, N, M,** and **H** on guidelines on the chalkboard. Ask children to name things they could buy that begin with each letter. Say the stroke description as children write each letter.

for visual learners
Have children choose a letter from a list on the chalkboard (**U, S, B, P, R, N, M, H**). Ask them to circle their letter and to demonstrate the correct way to write it.

for kinesthetic learners
Draw a large box with eight sections on the chalkboard. Write **u, s, b, p, r, n, m,** or **h** in each box. Have children take turns tossing a chalkboard eraser at the boxes, naming the letter the eraser hits and writing the letter on the chalkboard.

What the research says . . .

When we teach and value handwriting, we are sending a message to students and parents that we value legibility, attention to detail, neatness, correctness, and excellence.

—Reggie Routman, *Literacy at the Crossroads: Crucial Talk About Reading, Writing, and Other Teaching Dilemmas.* © Heinemann

Note: Correct body position, proper paper placement, and correct positioning of the writing implement are key factors for legibility. Encourage children to check these factors often as they write.

Support Materials

These support products and materials, which can foster practice and evaluation, are available in the **Handwriting** section of the Zaner-Bloser catalog.

- *Home Handwriting Pack*
- *Handwriting Evaluation Stamp*
- *Write-On, Wipe-Off Practice Boards*
- *Wipe-Off Practice Cards*

See the **Keys to Legibility Poster** *for more information.*

T69

Touch the midline; **pull down straight; curve forward** (right); **push up** to the midline. **Pull down straight** to the baseline.

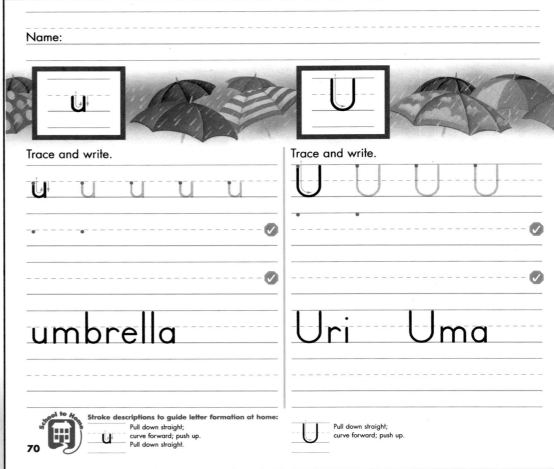

Name:

Trace and write.

u U U U U

✓

✓

umbrella

Trace and write.

U U U U

✓

✓

Uri Uma

School to Home Stroke descriptions to guide letter formation at home:
u Pull down straight;
curve forward; push up.
Pull down straight.
70

U Pull down straight;
curve forward; push up.

1. Present the Letter

Have the children look at lower-case **u**. Help them see the two pull down straight strokes and the connecting curve.

Model Write **u** on guidelines as you say the stroke description. Invite the children to use an index finger to write **u** on their desktop. Have them say the description with you as they write.

Practice Let the children practice writing **u** on marker boards or slates or on other paper before they write on the pages.

2. Write and Evaluate

Ask the children to trace the shaded letters with pencil, beginning each one at the dot. Then ask them to write two rows of letters and the word with **u**.

✓ **Stop and Check** This icon directs the children to stop and circle their best letter.

To help them evaluate **u,** ask:
• Are your pull down strokes straight?
• Does the curve of your **u** rest on the baseline?

Repeat teaching steps 1 and 2 for uppercase U.

To help children evaluate **U,** ask:
• Are your pull down and push up strokes straight?
• Is the curve of your **U** round?

Corrective Strategy

To help the children write **U** with vertical strokes, check the paper position. Then draw a dotted line across **U** to show where the curve forward stroke begins and ends. Have the children trace the letter.

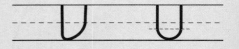

School to Home

Families may use the stroke descriptions on the student page to encourage good letter formation at home. Copy and distribute **Practice Master 96** for children to take home for more practice.

Write the words.

uncle   us   under   up

Write the sentence.

Use your umbrella now.

On Your Own Tell what you use when it rains.

Spacing
Circle two letters with good spacing between them.

71

Touch the headline; **pull down straight; curve forward** (right); **push up** to the headline.

Fun and Games

auditory   visual   kinesthetic

Railroad Warm-Up

Model a simple drawing of a railroad scene on the chalkboard that children may copy for a quick warm-up for writing. Use horizontal and vertical lines to form a train track and railroad car, circle lines to form wheels, and slant lines to form cross braces on the car's door. Challenge children to think of other warm-up drawings with the four basic manuscript strokes.

Tic-Tac-U Fold lined paper into nine boxes and write a tic-tac-toe grid in each. Pair children and ask them to use **u** and **U** to play the game, instead of **X** and **O**. Suggest that each child use a different color to write. Children will play this game in the traditional way, trying to complete a vertical, horizontal, or diagonal row to win.

Apply

Before the children write the words and sentence on the page, call attention to the spacing of the letters in all the words. Observe the children as they complete the page and respond to **On Your Own**.

Spacing

Help the children evaluate the spacing of their writing by comparing it with the models. Explain that there should be about the width of an index finger or the end of a narrow craft stick between words in a sentence. Then have them respond to the direction in the Key feature at the bottom of the page.

PRACTICE MASTERS 47–48

Name:

Write the letter and the words.

u u u u u u u u u

use   until   ugly   unite

bug   upset   untie

Copyright © Zaner-Bloser, Inc.   Practice Master 47

Una is in Utah.

Practice Master 48   Copyright © Zaner-Bloser, Inc.

Coaching Hint

Forming Letters If children have difficulty writing a specific letter, use chalk to write the letter in a large size on the playground pavement. Ask children to walk or hop along the letter in the correct sequence to reinforce good letter formation. (kinesthetic)

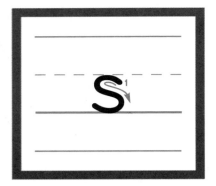

Touch below the midline; **curve back** (left); **curve forward** (right), ending above the baseline.

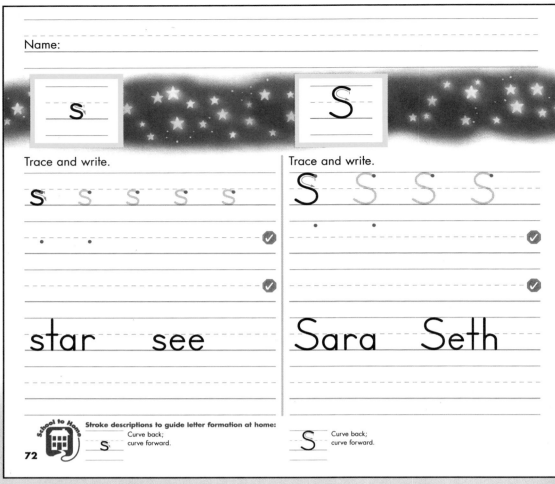

Name:

Trace and write.

S S S S S

star   see

Trace and write.

S S S S

Sara Seth

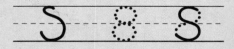

Stroke descriptions to guide letter formation at home:

S Curve back;
curve forward.

S Curve back;
curve forward.

1. Present the Letter

Direct the children to look at lowercase **s**. Focus attention on the letter's shape by pointing out the round top and bottom.

Model Write **s** on guidelines as you say the stroke description. Give each child half a pipe cleaner to form into an **s**. Have the children say the stroke description with you as they use their index finger to trace the **s**.

Practice Let the children practice writing **s** on marker boards or slates or on other paper before they write on the pages.

2. Write and Evaluate

Ask the children to trace the shaded letters with pencil, beginning each one at the dot. Then ask them to write two rows of letters and the words with **s**.

✓ **Stop and Check** This icon directs the children to stop and circle their best letter.

To help them evaluate **s**, ask:
- Does your **s** begin below the midline?
- Are the spaces in the top and bottom of your **s** similar?

*Repeat teaching steps 1 and 2 for uppercase **S**.*

To help children evaluate **S**, ask:
- Is the top of your **S** about the same size as the bottom?
- Is the width of your **S** about the same as the model?

Corrective Strategy

To help the children write the top and bottom of **S** the same width, draw one circle above another circle as shown and outline the backward and forward curves of **S** that form part of a circle. Make other sets of circles and have the children use them to write **S**.

S 8 S

Families may use the stroke descriptions on the student page to encourage good letter formation at home. Copy and distribute **Practice Master 97** for children to take home for more practice.

T72

Write the words.

seal   sun   sit   sell

Write the sentence.

Should I sing a song?

On Your Own Write the name of a song you like to sing.

Touch below the headline;
curve back (left); **curve forward** (right), ending above
the baseline.

Spacing

Circle two words with
good spacing between them.

73

Apply

Before the children write the
words and sentence on the page,
call attention to the spacing of the
letters in the words and of the
words in the sentence. Write
should correctly on the chalkboard, and then write it again
with the letters spaced incorrectly.
Discuss which model is correct
and why. Observe the children as
they complete the page and
respond to **On Your Own**.

Spacing

Help the children evaluate the
spacing of the letters they wrote
by comparing them with the
models. Then have them respond
to the direction in the Key feature
at the bottom of the page.

PRACTICE MASTERS 49–50

Name:

Write the letter and the words.

s   s   s   s   s   s   s

sleep   salt   seat   still

sad   same   seed   shoe

Copyright © Zaner-Bloser, Inc.   **Practice Master 49**

Sally is at Sid's house.

Practice Master 50   Copyright © Zaner-Bloser, Inc.

Coaching Hint

Left-Handed Writers When
working one-on-one with left-handed
writers, suggest that they hold their
pencils slightly farther back (about ½
inch above the raw wood). This
allows them to see what they are
writing. (visual, kinesthetic)

Fun and Games

auditory   visual   kinesthetic

Silly Snakes Provide clay
for children to roll between
their hands and then shape
into a long, long silly snake
and a short, short silly snake.
Compare the sizes. Ask them
to say /s/ as in *snake*. Have
them repeat the activity, this
time forming the letters **s** and
S. Compare the sizes. Have
the children use their finger
to trace over the completed
letters several times.

Surprise! Prepare a surprise
box with a set of textured
alphabet letters. You may wish
to use only the letters introduced so far. Have a volunteer, with eyes closed, pull a
letter from the box, trace it
with a finger, and try to name
the letter. Continue until all
the letters have been named.

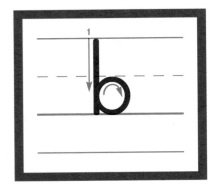

Touch the headline; **pull down straight** to the baseline. **Push up; circle forward** (right) all the way around.

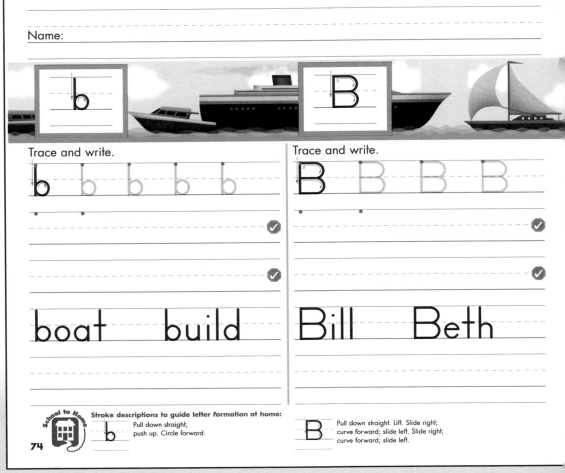

Name:

Trace and write.

b b b b b

boat   build

Trace and write.

B B B B

Bill   Beth

School to Home   Stroke descriptions to guide letter formation at home:
 Pull down straight; push up. Circle forward.

B Pull down straight. Lift. Slide right; curve forward; slide left. Slide right; curve forward; slide left.

74

1. Present the Letter

Have the children look at lowercase **b**. Point out how **b** fits between the headline and the baseline.

Model Write **b** on guidelines as you say the stroke description. Have the children use their finger to trace the model **b** in their books as you repeat the description.

Practice Let the children practice writing **b** on marker boards or slates or on other paper before they write on the pages.

2. Write and Evaluate

Ask the children to trace the shaded letters with pencil, beginning each one at the dot. Then ask them to write two rows of letters and the words with **b**.

Stop and Check This icon directs the children to stop and circle their best letter.

To help them evaluate **b**, ask:
- Does your **b** begin at the headline?
- Is your forward circle round?

Repeat teaching steps 1 and 2 for uppercase B.

To help children evaluate **B**, ask:
- Are the curves of your **B** round?
- Is your **B** about the same width as the model?

Corrective Strategy

To help the children write **B** with correct proportion, call attention to the retracing at the midline. Also remind the children to make their slide right and slide left strokes the same width.

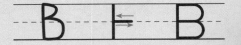

Families may use the stroke descriptions on the student page to encourage good letter formation at home. Copy and distribute **Practice Master 98** for children to take home for more practice.

Write the words.

bell baby bake bring

Write the sentence.

Big books are great!

On Your Own Tell what kind of books you like.

Spacing
Circle two letters with good spacing between them.

75

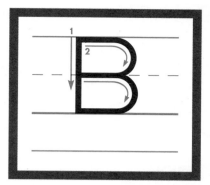

Touch the headline; **pull down straight** to the baseline. Lift. Touch the headline; **slide right; curve forward** (right) to the midline; **slide left**. **Slide right; curve forward** (right) to the baseline. **Slide left**.

Fun and Games

auditory visual kinesthetic

Apply

Before the children write the words and sentence on the page, write the sentence on the chalkboard, making several obvious errors in the spacing of some of the letters in the words and between words in the sentence. Read the sentence and ask if it is written correctly. Elicit that some of the spacing is incorrect. Observe the children as they complete the page and respond to **On Your Own**.

Spacing

Help the children evaluate the spacing of the letters they wrote by comparing them with the models. Then have them respond to the direction in the Key feature at the bottom of the page.

PRACTICE MASTERS 51–52

Name:

Write the letter and the words.

b b b b b b b b

bug   bat   boss   bill

bean   bark   big   bee

Copyright © Zaner-Bloser, Inc.   Practice Master 51

Bruno biked to Boise.

Practice Master 52   Copyright © Zaner-Bloser, Inc.

Coaching Hint

Reversals Show the children how to hold up their fists, with the backs of the hands facing away and the thumbs pointing up. The resulting hand shapes can serve as a convenient reminder of the difference between **b** and **d**. Emphasize the different starting points for writing these two frequently confused letters. (visual, kinesthetic)

Phonics Connection

Say *brown bear* and help children note that both *brown* and *bear* begin with the /b/ sound. Read pairs of words such as these: *black bear; red bear; baby bear; mother bear; big bear; friendly bear.* For each pair, ask if the words begin alike. If they do, have a volunteer write **b** on guidelines on the chalkboard.

Letter Bingo Help children make a board for this letter game by dividing writing paper into sixteen boxes. Invite children to write one uppercase or one lowercase letter in each box. Make a set of letter cards for the caller. To play, choose a letter card, call the letter, and have players cover it with a marker if it is on their board.

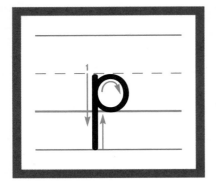

Touch the midline; **pull down straight** through the baseline to the next guideline. **Push up; circle forward** (right) all the way around.

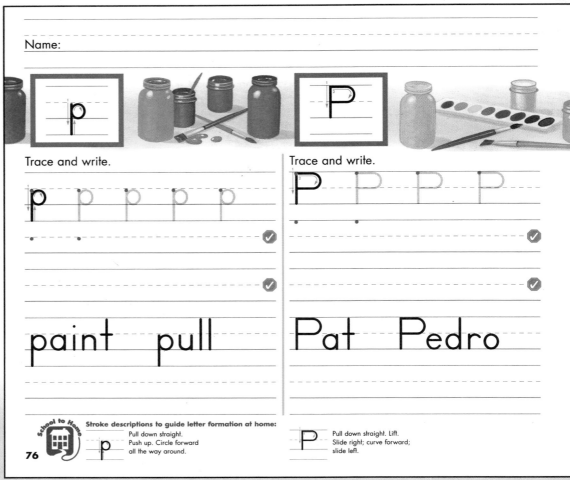

Name:

Trace and write.

p p p p p

paint pull

Trace and write.

P P P P

Pat Pedro

School to Home

Stroke descriptions to guide letter formation at home:

Pull down straight.
Push up. Circle forward
all the way around.

Pull down straight. Lift.
Slide right; curve forward;
slide left.

76

1. Present the Letter

Direct the children to look at lowercase **p**. Help them recognize that **p** rests on the baseline and descends to the line below.

Model Write **p** on guidelines as you say the stroke description. Model writing **p** in the air as you repeat the description. Have the children say the names of the strokes as they write **p** in the air with you.

Practice Let the children practice writing **p** on marker boards or slates or on other paper before they write on the pages.

2. Write and Evaluate

Ask the children to trace the shaded letters with pencil, beginning each one at the dot. Then ask them to write two rows of letters and the words with **p**.

Stop and Check This icon directs children to stop and circle their best letter.

To help them evaluate **p**, ask:
- Is your forward circle round?
- Is your **p** straight up and down?

Repeat teaching steps 1 and 2 for uppercase P.

To help children evaluate **P**, ask:
- Are your slide right and slide left strokes the same width?
- Is your **P** about the same width as the model?

Corrective Strategy

To help the children make a round forward circle, make a pull down straight stroke that touches the next guideline; then place a dot about halfway between the midline and baseline. Say the stroke description as the children trace and write **p**.

P P P

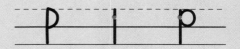

School to Home

Families may use the stroke descriptions on the student page to encourage good letter formation at home. Copy and distribute **Practice Master 99** for students to take home for more practice.

Write the words.

pen   pig   push   put

Write the sentence.

Please pass the paper.

On Your Own Write a sentence that begins with **Please**.

Spacing

Circle two words with
good spacing between them.

77

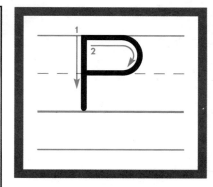

Touch the headline; **pull
down straight** to the baseline. Lift. Touch the headline;
slide right; curve forward
(right) to the midline; **slide
left**.

Fun and Games

auditory   visual   kinesthetic

Phonics Connection

Provide finger paint and
paper. Allow time for the children to experiment with writing letters. Then ask what letter begins *pig*. After children
agree that *pig* begins with **p,**
have them write **p** when they
hear a word that begins like
pig. Say words that do and do
not begin with **p**. Repeat with
names of people for **P**.

Pig Latin
Explain that pig
Latin is a fun language children can use. To speak pig
Latin, they should take the
first sound of a word off the
beginning and add it to the
end. Then add an **ay** sound.
Ig-pay is **pig** in pig Latin.
Encourage them to try saying
and writing their names in pig
Latin. Invite them to translate
other words and sentences
into pig Latin.

3 Apply

Before the children write the
words and sentence on the
page, call attention to the
spacing in the writing. Remind
them that good spacing makes
their writing easi-
er to read. Observe the children
as they complete the page and
respond to **On Your Own**.

Spacing

Help the children evaluate the
spacing of the letters they wrote
by comparing them with the
models. Then have them respond
to the direction in the Key feature
at the bottom of the page.

PRACTICE MASTERS 53–54

Name:

Write the letter and the words.

p p p p p p p p p

pop party pup paper

pat page pet pretty

Copyright © Zaner-Bloser, Inc.   Practice Master 53

Polly paddled to Peru.

Practice Master 54   Copyright © Zaner-Bloser, Inc.

Coaching Hint

Hands-On Handwriting

Prepare tactile letters, such as sandpaper letters, or use Zaner-Bloser's
Touch and Trace Letter Cards. Have
the children close their eyes, touch a
letter, and identify it by its size and
shape. You may need to guide a
child's direction in exploring letter
shape. (kinesthetic)

T77

Practice and Application

Practice

Write the letters.

u u u   s s s   b b b   p p p

U U   S S   B B   P P

Write the words.

bus   pup   cub   cup

78

1. Review the Letters

Direct the children to look at the letters being reviewed on student page 78. Ask them what they remember about correct spacing. (*Leave about the width of a finger or a narrow craft stick between words; follow the models for spacing between letters in a word.*)

Review the stroke descriptions and model again any of the letters the children may be having difficulty writing.

Ask a volunteer to give a verbal description of one of these letters: **u, s, b, p, U, S, B, P**. Challenge the other children to identify the letter being described and then write it on guidelines on the chalkboard.

2. Write and Evaluate

Tell the children to write the letters, beginning each one at the proper starting point. Then have them write the words on the page. Remind children to form their letters carefully and refer to the models often so their writing will have correct spacing and be easy to read.

Stop and Check

To help children evaluate their lowercase letters, ask:

- Does **u** begin at the midline?
- Are the top and bottom of your **s** similar?
- Are the circle forward strokes in your **b** and **p** round?

To help children evaluate their uppercase letters, ask:

- Does your **S** begin below the headline?
- Do your **U, B,** and **P** begin with a pull down straight stroke?

Corrective Strategy

To help the children write **s** or **S** correctly, make two dotted circles, one on top of the other, and then outline the curves.

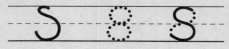

More About Practice

The quality of handwriting practice is more important than the quantity. Asking children to write letters many times without stopping to evaluate can reinforce bad habits and lead to sloppy, rushed work. Instead, have students write a letter several times and then circle their best attempt.

T78

Application Write the tongue twisters. Then say them fast.

Bob bakes bread.

Paula pets a pink pig.

Six snakes have snacks.

My Words

Spacing
Circle a word you wrote that has good spacing.

79

Sing! Sing! Sing!
Brainstorm names of familiar children's songs. Then ask the children to write two of their favorites on handwriting paper. Collect the papers, and help volunteers write the lyrics to the songs on chart paper so the children can follow along as they sing. Sing a few songs each day until all their favorites have been sung.

Apply

Before children write the tongue twisters, ask volunteers to look at student page 79 and describe what they remember about spacing. Remind them to write with correct spacing. Observe children as they write on the page.

My Words Ask children to write tongue twister words of their own. Encourage them to write words that contain the review letters. If they need help, suggest they look for words on the previous pages.

 **Spacing**

Help children summarize what they have learned about spacing. Then have them respond to the direction in the Key feature.

Special Helps

To foster control of the fingers, try this activity. When children are using markers, challenge them to cap and uncap the markers using only the writing hand. When they have finished using a marker, have them move or "inchworm" the marker through the hand to retrieve the marker cap from the back of the marker. Then ask them to move the marker back through the hand to snap on the cap until they hear the "click."

To strengthen hand arches, make sure children are using their fingertips, and not pressing down on their palms or desktops, to cap the marker.

—*Maureen King, O.T.R.*

Fun and Games

 auditory   visual   kinesthetic

Set the Table Ask the children to imagine they are inviting guests for lunch and that they want to set the table correctly. Distribute large sheets of manila paper and crayons. Tell the children that the paper represents a place mat, and they will help set the table by drawing what is needed. Demonstrate at the chalkboard. Ask children to draw a plate in the center of the mat. Then ask them to draw a fork to the left of the plate and a knife and a spoon to the right of the plate.

T79

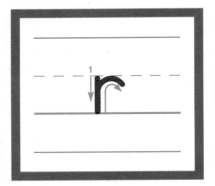

Touch the midline; **pull down straight** to the baseline. **Push up; curve forward** (right).

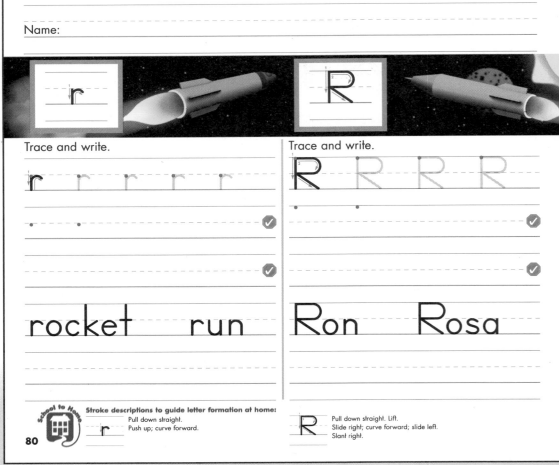

Name:

Trace and write.

r r r r r

rocket   run

Trace and write.

R R R R

Ron   Rosa

School to Home
Stroke descriptions to guide letter formation at home:
r — Pull down straight. Push up; curve forward.
R — Pull down straight. Lift. Slide right; curve forward; slide left. Slant right.

80

1. Present the Letter

Direct the children to look at lowercase **r**. Focus attention on the letter's shape by pointing out how the curve forward stroke begins and ends just below the midline.

Model Write **r** on guidelines as you say the stroke description. Have the children use their finger to write **r** on their desktop and repeat the description as you say it again.

Practice Let the children practice writing **r** on marker boards or slates or on other paper before they write on the pages.

2. Write and Evaluate

Ask the children to trace the shaded letters with pencil, beginning each one at the dot. Then ask them to write two rows of letters and the words with **r**.

 Stop and Check This icon directs the children to stop and circle their best letter.

To help them evaluate **r**, ask:
• Did you end your push up stroke at the right place?
• Does your curve forward stroke end below the midline?

*Repeat teaching steps 1 and 2 for uppercase **R**.*

To help children evaluate **R**, ask:
• Are your slide right and slide left strokes the same width?
• Does your slant right stroke touch the baseline?

Corrective Strategy

To help the children write a slant right stroke, demonstrate how to make the stroke from the midline to the baseline. Write **R**, omitting the slant right stroke. As you say the description, have the children trace and complete **R**.

School to Home
Families may use the stroke descriptions on the student page to encourage good letter formation at home. Copy and distribute **Practice Master 100** for children to take home for more practice.

Write the words.

rock   rain   read   ring

Write the sentence.

Read me a story.

On Your Own Tell who reads to you.

Spacing
Circle two letters with good spacing between them.

81

Touch the headline; **pull down straight** to the baseline. Lift. Touch the headline; **slide right; curve forward** (right) to the midline; **slide left**. **Slant right** to the baseline.

Fun and Games

Letter Riddles List these letters on the chalkboard: **r, p, b, s, u,** and **q.** Then say:

- *I am a letter with a descender.*
- *I have a circle forward stroke.*
- *I come after o in the alphabet.*

Which letter am I?

Ask more riddles and invite children to make up some riddles of their own.

Category Fun List these four categories on the chalkboard: *Girls' Names, Boys' Names, Food, Animals.* Invite children to brainstorm words that begin with **r** or **R** for each category. Write their responses and ask volunteers to trace over the letters **r** and **R** with colored chalk. Add other categories to extend the game.

Apply

Before the children write the words and sentence on the page, emphasize that correct spacing between letters in words and between words in sentences makes writing more legible. Observe the children as they complete the page and respond to **On Your Own**.

 Spacing

Help the children evaluate the spacing of the letters they wrote by comparing them with the models. Then have them respond to the direction in the Key feature at the bottom of the page.

PRACTICE MASTERS 55–56

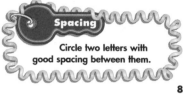

Name:

Write the letter and the words.

r r r r r r r

real   red   roll   road

rope   ride   room   right

Copyright © Zaner-Bloser, Inc.   Practice Master 55

Raj ran to Reno.

Practice Master 56   Copyright © Zaner-Bloser, Inc.

Coaching Hint

Positions for Writing When children are writing, call out "Freeze!" Children should then stop writing and freeze their positions. They should check their sitting, paper, and pencil positions and make any needed adjustments before they "thaw" and begin to write again. (auditory, visual, kinesthetic)

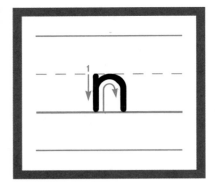

Touch the midline; **pull down straight** to the baseline. **Push up; curve forward** (right); **pull down straight** to the baseline.

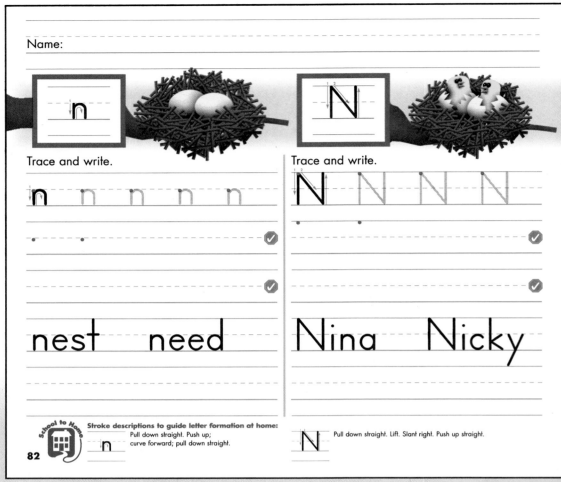

Name:

Trace and write.

n n n n n

nest   need

Trace and write.

N N N N

Nina   Nicky

School to Home

Stroke descriptions to guide letter formation at home:
 Pull down straight. Push up; curve forward; pull down straight.

N Pull down straight. Lift. Slant right. Push up straight.

1. Present the Letter

Have the children look at lower-case **n**. Focus attention on the letter's shape by pointing out its similarity to lowercase **r**.

Model Write **n** on guidelines as you say the stroke description. Model using your finger to write **n** on sandpaper or on the **n** card from Zaner-Bloser's *Touch and Trace Letter Cards*. Pair children and have them take turns following your model of writing with their fingers and saying the description.

Practice Let the children practice writing **n** on marker boards or slates or on other paper before they write on the pages.

2. Write and Evaluate

Ask the children to trace the shaded letters with pencil, beginning each one at the dot. Then ask them to write two rows of letters and the words with **n**.

Stop and Check This icon directs the children to stop and circle their best letter.

To help them evaluate **n,** ask:
• Does your **n** touch the midline and the baseline?
• Is your **n** straight up and down?

Repeat teaching steps 1 and 2 for uppercase N.

To help children evaluate **N,** ask:
• Does your push up straight stroke end at the headline?
• Is your **N** about the same width as the model?

Corrective Strategy

To help the children write **N** the correct width, place dots as shown and ask them to write the letter as you say the stroke description. Call attention to the width of the slant line, and suggest that children try to make their slant lines the same width.

School to Home

Families may use the stroke descriptions on the student page to encourage good letter formation at home. Copy and distribute **Practice Master 101** for children to take home for more practice.

Write the words.

nine   nail   nap   nod

Write the sentences.

No napping! Wake up!

On Your Own Tell at what time you wake up.

Spacing
Circle two words with good spacing between them.

83

Touch the headline; **pull down straight** to the baseline. Lift. Touch the headline; **slant right** to the baseline. **Push up straight** to the headline.

Fun and Games

Apply

Before the children write the words and sentences on the page, emphasize that correct spacing is an important part of legible handwriting. Explain that they should leave about the width of an index finger or the end of a narrow craft stick between words in a sentence and twice that amount of space between sentences. Observe the children as they complete the page and respond to **On Your Own**.

Spacing

Help the children evaluate the spacing of the letters they wrote by comparing them with the models. Then have them respond to the direction in the Key feature at the bottom of the page.

PRACTICE MASTERS 57–58

Coaching Hint

Size Demonstrate for children the technique of drawing a horizontal line with a ruler along the tops of their letters to show proper and consistent size. Have them use this technique to evaluate the size of their letters, especially when they are writing on paper without guidelines. (visual)

Noodle-bets Collect and display different-shaped pastas and have children describe the shapes. Point out shapes that are straight up and down or that have circles. Invite children to use the shapes to form alphabet or "noodle-bet" letters.

Phonics Connection

Write *noon* in large letters on the chalkboard. Point out that *noon* begins and ends with **n**. Print words such as these on cards: *nice, nose, fan, pin, hen, night*. Ask children to listen for the beginning and ending sounds as you read each word. If the word begins like *noon*, have a child tape the word under the initial **n** on the chalkboard. If it ends like *noon*, have a child tape the word under the final **n**.

T83

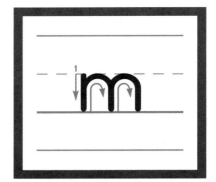

Touch the midline; **pull down straight** to the baseline. **Push up; curve forward** (right); **pull down straight** to the baseline. **Push up; curve forward** (right); **pull down straight** to the baseline.

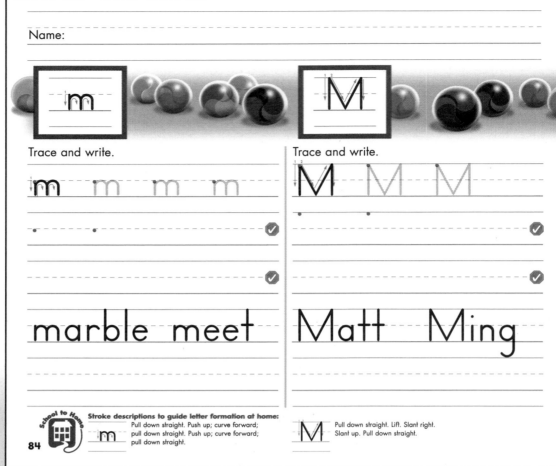

Name:

Trace and write.

m m m m

marble meet

Trace and write.

M M M

Matt Ming

School to Home

Stroke descriptions to guide letter formation at home:

Pull down straight. Push up; curve forward; pull down straight. Push up; curve forward; pull down straight.

Pull down straight. Lift. Slant right. Slant up. Pull down straight.

84

Have the children look at lowercase **m**. Focus attention on the letter's shape by pointing out that **m** has three pull down straight strokes and two curve forward strokes.

Model Write **m** on guidelines as you say the stroke description. In turn, ask the children to dip their finger into water and write **m** on the chalkboard as they say the description together.

Practice Let the children practice writing **m** on marker boards or slates or on other paper before they write on the pages.

2. Write and Evaluate

Ask the children to trace the shaded letters with pencil, beginning each one at the dot. Then ask them to write two rows of letters and the words with **m**.

Stop and Check This icon directs children to stop and circle their best letter.

To help them evaluate **m**, ask:
- Does your **m** have three pull down straight strokes?
- Are the tops of the curve strokes round?

Repeat teaching steps 1 and 2 for uppercase M.

To help students evaluate **M,** ask:
- Does your **M** rest on the baseline?
- Is your **M** about the same width as the model?

Corrective Strategy

To help the children make **M** the correct width, place dots as shown. Say the strokes and have the children connect the dots, lifting the pencil only once, after the first stroke.

Families may use the stroke descriptions on the student page to encourage good letter formation at home. Copy and distribute **Practice Master 102** for students to take home for more practice.

Write the words.

mom   moon   mail   miss

Write the sentence.

My lunch is yummy!

On Your Own Tell what you like for lunch.

Spacing

Circle two letters with good spacing between them.

85

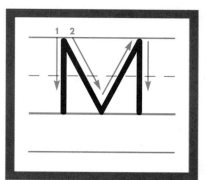

Touch the headline; **pull down straight** to the baseline. Lift. Touch the headline; **slant right** to the baseline. **Slant up** (right) to the headline. **Pull down straight** to the baseline.

Fun and Games

auditory   visual   kinesthetic

Silly Sentences Invite children to help you write silly sentences about monkeys. Use several words that begin with the same sound. Pair children and let them work together. Here are some examples to get you started: *Monkeys munch on marvelous muffins. Monkeys march merrily in May.*

Monkey See and Do Choose a volunteer to be the "monkey" of the moment. Ask the child to write **m** or **M** on guidelines on the chalkboard. Then ask the "monkey" to choose another child to "see and do" the same. As the game continues, select different children to take the roles, and encourage the "monkey" to write words as well as letters.

3 Apply

Before the children write the words and sentence on the page, point out the correct spacing in the writing. Encourage the children to write their letters carefully, using good letter and word spacing. Observe the children as they complete the page and respond to **On Your Own**.

Spacing

Help the children evaluate the spacing of the letters they wrote by comparing them with the models. Then have them respond to the direction in the Key feature at the bottom of the page.

PRACTICE MASTERS 59–60

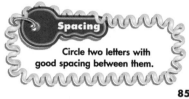

Name:

Write the letter and the words.

m   m   m   m   m   m   m

meal   made   middle   miss

moo   must   make   may

Copyright © Zaner-Bloser, Inc.   Practice Master 59

Mario misses Mrs. Mack

Practice Master 60   Copyright © Zaner-Bloser, Inc.

Coaching Hint

Slant Children can evaluate the vertical quality of their handwriting by making sure their paper is positioned properly and then drawing pencil lines through the vertical strokes of their letters. If the lines are parallel, the vertical quality is correct. (visual)

T85

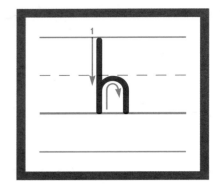

Touch the headline; **pull down straight** to the baseline. **Push up; curve forward** (right); **pull down straight** to the baseline.

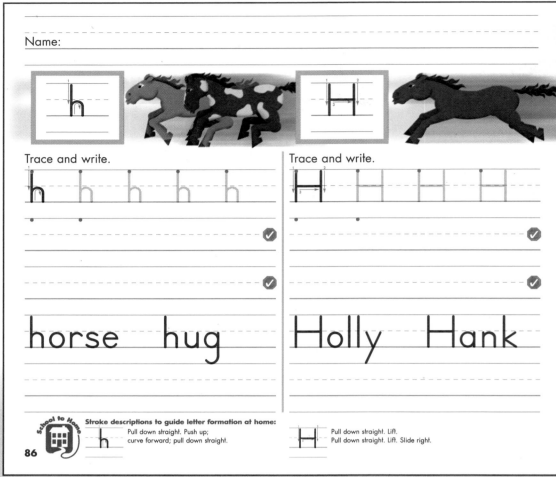

Name:

Trace and write.

h h h h h

✓

✓

horse hug

Trace and write.

H H H H H

✓

✓

Holly Hank

🏫 **Stroke descriptions to guide letter formation at home:**

h Pull down straight. Push up; curve forward; pull down straight.

H Pull down straight. Lift. Pull down straight. Lift. Slide right.

86

1. Present the Letter

Have the children look at lower-case **h**. Focus attention on the letter's shape by asking children to name other letters they see in **h**.

Model Write **h** on guidelines as you say the stroke description. Have the children use their finger to trace the model **h** in their books as you repeat the stroke description. Then have them say the stroke description with you as they trace **h** again.

Practice Let the children practice writing **h** on marker boards or slates or on other paper before they write on the pages.

2. Write and Evaluate

Ask the children to trace the shaded letters with pencil, beginning each one at the dot. Then ask them to write two rows of letters and the words with **h**.

✓ **Stop and Check** This icon directs children to stop and circle their best letter.

To help them evaluate **h,** ask:

- Are your pull down straight strokes straight?
- Does your **h** touch the headline and baseline?

Repeat teaching steps 1 and 2 for uppercase H.

To help children evaluate **H,** ask:

- Is your **H** straight up and down?
- Is your slide right stroke on the midline?

Corrective Strategy

To help the children begin and end the forward curve of **h** correctly, write **h** and put a dot at the start and end of the curve. Remind the children to make straight vertical lines on both sides of the curve forward stroke.

Families may use the stroke descriptions on the student page to encourage good letter formation at home. Copy and distribute **Practice Master 103** for students to take home for more practice.

Write the words.

hill   house   have   hop

Write the sentence.

How can I help you?

On Your Own   Tell how you help others.

Spacing

Circle two words with good spacing between them.

87

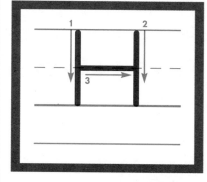

Touch the headline; **pull down straight** to the base-line. Lift. Move to the right and touch the headline; **pull down straight** to the base-line. Lift. Move to the left and touch the midline; **slide right**.

Fun and Games

auditory   visual   kinesthetic

Hungry Hippo Introduce this game by describing a hungry hippo you know who will eat almost anything. Start the game, and soon the children will be able to join in. *I know a hippo who loves to eat. He eats hens, but he never eats chickens. He eats hats, but he never eats socks.* Children should quickly discover that Hippo likes words that begin with **h**.

Letters-Within-Letters
Ask children to examine the alphabet and find letters-within-letters. For example, **o** is found in **a, d, g,** and **q; r** is found in **h, m,** and **n.** Have children practice writing letters-within-letters or shaping them with clay.

Apply

Before the children write the words and sentence on the page, ask them how they know where one word ends and another begins. Help them discover that the spaces between words are the same width, about as wide as an index finger. Observe the children as they complete the page and respond to **On Your Own**. After they write on the page, guide them to recognize why one word might have better spacing than another.

Spacing

Help the children evaluate the spacing of the letters they wrote by comparing them with the models. Then have them respond to the direction in the Key feature at the bottom of the page.

PRACTICE MASTERS 61–62

Name:

Write the letter and the words.

h h h h h h h h

hen   hush   hand   hot

had   has   hurt   hat

Copyright © Zaner-Bloser, Inc.   Practice Master 61

Hilary is here in Haiti.

Practice Master 62   Copyright © Zaner-Bloser, Inc.

Coaching Hint

Letter Formation Having children use their index finger to trace Zaner-Bloser's *Touch and Trace Letter Cards* or a set of sandpaper letters can provide kinesthetic reinforcement of letter formation. Saying the strokes as they trace the letters adds auditory reinforcement. (kinesthetic, auditory)

T87

Practice and Application

1. Review the Letters

Direct the children to look at the letters being reviewed on student page 88. Ask them what they remember about the spacing between letters and between words. (*Follow the models to learn correct spacing between letters; leave about the width of a finger or a narrow craft stick between words.*)

Review the stroke descriptions and model again any of the letters the children may be having difficulty writing.

Ask a volunteer to give a verbal description of one of these letters: **r, n, m, h, R, N, M, H**. Challenge the other children to identify the letter being described and then write it on guidelines on the chalkboard.

2. Write and Evaluate

Have the children write the letters, beginning each one at the proper starting point. Then have them write the words on the page. Remind children to refer to the models often and to leave the correct amount of space between letters.

Stop and Check

To help children evaluate their lowercase letters, ask:

- Does the curve forward in your **r** end below the midline?
- Are the pull down straight strokes in your **n** and **m** vertical?
- Is your **h** written between the headline and baseline?

To help children evaluate their uppercase letters, ask:

- Are your **R** and **M** about the same width as the models?
- Does your **N** rest on the baseline?
- Are your strokes in **H** straight?

Corrective Strategy

To help the children write **m,** remind them to push up (retrace) carefully to avoid making loops.

 not

More About Practice

Handwriting practice is most beneficial when done in the child's primary learning modality. Kinesthetic learners might form letters with blocks or write large letters on the chalkboard. Auditory learners may write letters as they listen to a recording of the stroke descriptions. Visual learners will benefit from writing directly under a model you have prepared.

T88

Application   Write the list of things to do.

1. Return Nate's hat.

2. Make a map.

3. Have a snack.

Spacing

Circle a word you wrote that has good spacing.

89

Write Away

Wish Lists Since wish lists are something children may enjoy writing, ask the children to think about wishes and to write a wish list of things they might wish to do or see, as on a summer vacation. Talk about the things they might include. After the lists are completed, ask volunteers to share their lists.

Apply

Before children write the to-do items on student page 89, ask volunteers to look at the page and tell what they notice about spacing. Remind them to use proper spacing so their words will be easy to read. Observe children as they write on the page.

Spacing

Help children summarize what they have learned about spacing. Then have them respond to the direction in the Key feature.

Special Helps

To foster eye-hand coordination and provide an alternative skill builder for writing development, prepare cards with patterns of prewriting strokes or simple shapes; for example, OTOTOTO, △△△, or □□□. Ask the child to use a writing implement or his or her index finger to trace over the lines of each shape.

Alternatively, provide stencils of basic shapes. Ask pairs to work together to create shape patterns using the stencils.

—*Maureen King, O.T.R.*

Fun and Games

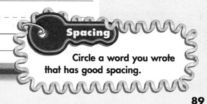

auditory   visual   kinesthetic

Letters in Color Have the children practice writing **u, s, b, p, U, S, B,** and **P** using paints and cotton swabs. Ask them to form letters as you say the stroke descriptions. Then have the children say the stroke descriptions as classmates write the letters. Expand the activity by including other letters the children have learned.

Featured Letters

vV yY wW

xX kK zZ

Featured Key to Legibility:

Slant

In manuscript writing, letters are written with vertical slant. Positioning the paper correctly and pulling strokes in the proper direction will help children write vertical letters.

Other Acceptable Letterforms

The following letterforms are acceptable variations of the models shown in this book.

k kK W

Alternate Letter Formation

Use these stroke descriptions to show an alternate method for children who have difficulty using the continuous-stroke method.

V — **Slant right**. Lift. **Slant left**.

W — **Slant right**. Lift. **Slant left**. Lift. **Slant right**. Lift. **Slant left** to the baseline.

Keys to Legibility

Make your writing easy to read. Look at the slant of the letters.

Slant

This writing is straight up and down.

Hello, everyone!

This writing is easy to read.

These letters are straight up and down.

straight

90

---

1. Present the Key

Point out the Key feature at the top of student page 90. It directs them to consider the vertical slant of their writing.

Direct the children to look at the greeting and at the letters and rabbits below it. Help them recognize the vertical quality being shown.

Have children read the directions and look at the two rows of words at the top of student page 91. Guide them in identifying which words are written with consistent verticality.

On guidelines on the chalkboard, write words with inconsistent vertical quality. Provide another set of guidelines under the first set. Have volunteers choose a word, identify letters that are not vertical, and then write the word correctly.

2. Trace and Evaluate

Read the directions for the trace-and-write activity on student page 91. Encourage children to trace and then write the letters in each word. Guide them in evaluating their writing by asking questions such as these:

- Are your strokes smooth and even?
- Are your letters about the same width as the models?
- Do all your letters rest on the baseline?
- Did you write letters that are straight up and down?

Circle each word that is straight up and down.

smile   smile   *smile*   sm\le

laugh   \augh   laugh   laugh

Trace and write words. Make the letters straight up and down.

giggle   sing   dance

hum   play

91

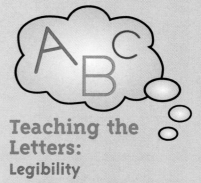

Teaching the Letters:
Legibility

The teacher may help the children transfer good handwriting to writing in the content areas by recognizing and valuing legibility in all written work. When their handwriting is regularly evaluated, children will begin to make a habit of remembering the four keys —shape, size, spacing, and slant—whenever they write. As they gain automaticity in their handwriting, children are free to focus on what they want to communicate, rather than on the mechanics of handwriting.

Meeting Individual Needs

for auditory learners
Provide guidelines on the chalkboard and have volunteers write a letter as you name the strokes in the letter. Direct the children to pay close attention to the terms used for the strokes.

for visual learners
Write **v, V, y, Y, w, W, x, X, k, K, z,** and **Z** on the chalkboard. Ask a volunteer to choose two of the letters to use for a comparison. Ask: How are these letters alike? Different? Which strokes are the same? Which has the most strokes?

for kinesthetic learners
In an open area in the classroom, invite children to "walk out" each letter, forming it on the floor by walking its shape.

What the research says . . .

Many children lack the eye-hand coordination to transfer what they see in the distance to what they write on paper, and they seem to perform better when the model is close to them, perhaps on each child's desk.

—Elinor P. Ross and Betty D. Roe, *Handwriting Instruction.*
© Wadsworth

Note: Writing their own work, especially for an audience, is often more meaningful to children than copying someone else's writing.

Support Materials
These support products and materials, which can facilitate practice and publication for young writers, are available in the **Handwriting** section of the Zaner-Bloser catalog.

✏ *Wipe-Off Practice Cards*
✏ *Zaner-Bloser Fontware*
✏ *Standard Pen*

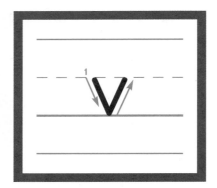

Touch the midline; **slant right** to the baseline. **Slant up** (right) to the midline.

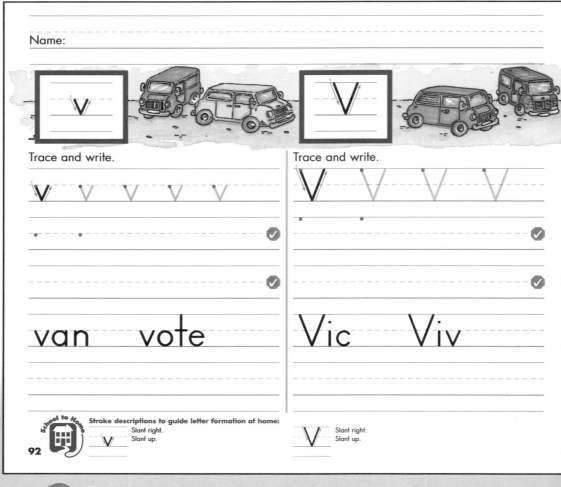

Name:

Trace and write.

V V V V V

van   vote

Trace and write.

V V V V

Vic   Viv

Stroke descriptions to guide letter formation at home:

V Slant right.
Slant up.

V Slant right.
Slant up.

---

1. Present the Letter

Direct children to look at lower-case **v**. Point out that **v** has two slant strokes that meet at the baseline.

Model Write **v** and **V** on guidelines as you say the stroke descriptions. Have the children compare the size and formation of the letters. Show them how to form a **v** by holding two fingers on a slant and tracing **v** as they say the description with you.

Practice Let the children practice writing **v** on marker boards or slates or on other paper before they write on the pages.

2. Write and Evaluate

Ask the children to trace the shaded letters with pencil, beginning each one at the dot. Then ask them to write two rows of letters and the words with **v**.

Stop and Check This icon directs the children to stop and circle their best letter.

To help them evaluate **v,** ask:
- Are your slant strokes straight?
- Does your **v** touch both the midline and baseline?

Repeat teaching steps 1 and 2 for uppercase V.

To help children evaluate **V,** ask:
- Are your strokes straight and not curved?
- Is your **V** about the same width as the model?

Corrective Strategy

To write **v** the correct width, place two dots on the midline and one on the baseline. Have the children connect the dots with the slant strokes as you say the description. Draw a dotted vertical line to show that the two sides of **v** are the same width.

V . . V

Families may use the stroke descriptions on the student page to encourage good letter formation at home. Copy and distribute **Practice Master 104** for children to take home for more practice.

Write the words.

vest   video   visit   very

Write the sentence.

Vera loves vegetables.

On Your Own Tell what you love to eat.

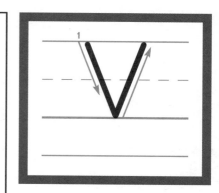

Touch the headline; **slant right** to the baseline. **Slant up** (right) to the headline.

Slant

Circle a letter that is straight up and down.

93

Fun and Games

auditory   visual   kinesthetic

What Is It? Paste one row of guidelines at the top of drawing paper. Ask the children to write *It is very, very* _____. Help them complete the sentence with an adjective of their choice. Then ask them to draw a picture to illustrate the sentence. Suggest they share their picture with a partner or a small group.

Vegetable Stew Ask children to help you make alphabet

3 Apply

Before the children write the words and sentence on the page, write *Vera* and *vest* on guidelines on the chalkboard. Have them compare the slant to the pull down straight strokes of the letters **r** and **t**. Observe the children as they complete the page and respond to **On Your Own**.

Slant

Help the children evaluate the vertical slant of the letters they wrote by comparing them with the models. Then have them respond to the direction in the Key feature at the bottom of the page.

PRACTICE MASTERS 63–64

Name:

Write the letter and the words.

V   V   V   V   V   V   V   V

voice   valley   van   vine

give   hive   vase   velvet

Copyright © Zaner-Bloser, Inc.   Practice Master 63

Vera visited Vermont.

Practice Master 64   Copyright © Zaner-Bloser, Inc.

Coaching Hint

Practice If children have not mastered a handwriting skill or stroke, provide additional instruction and practice. Reinforce instruction with activities geared to each child's modality strengths. Help them evaluate their writing.

they

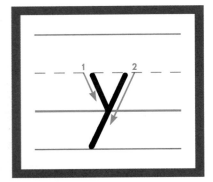

Touch the midline; **slant right** to the baseline. Lift. Move to the right and touch the midline; **slant left** through the baseline.

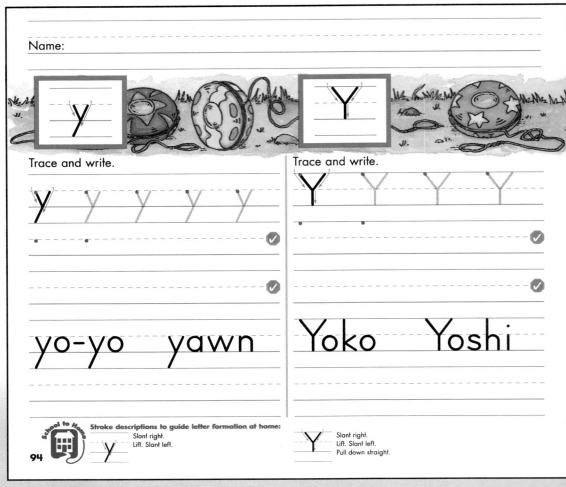

Name:

Trace and write.

y y y y y

yo-yo yawn

Trace and write.

Y Y Y Y Y

Yoko Yoshi

School to Home

94

Stroke descriptions to guide letter formation at home:

y   Slant right.
     Lift. Slant left.

Y   Slant right.
     Lift. Slant left.
     Pull down straight.

1. Present the Letter

Direct the children to look at lowercase **y**. Point out that like **v**, lowercase **y** has two slant strokes, but one of them goes below the baseline.

Model Write **y** on guidelines as you say the stroke description. Model writing **y** in the air as you repeat the description. Have the children say the names of the strokes as they write **y** in the air with you.

Practice Let the children practice writing **y** on marker boards or slates or on other paper before they write on the pages.

2. Write and Evaluate

Ask the children to trace the shaded letters with pencil, beginning each one at the dot. Then ask them to write two rows of letters and the words with **y**.

Stop and Check This icon directs the children to stop and circle their best letter.

To help them evaluate **y**, ask:
- Does your slant right stroke stop at the baseline?
- Does your **y** touch the headline of the next writing space?

Repeat teaching steps 1 and 2 for uppercase Y.

To help children evaluate **Y**, ask:
- Do your slant strokes meet at the midline?
- Are your strokes straight?

Corrective Strategy

To help the children see that **Y** is formed with two slant strokes and one pull down straight stroke, write three models of **Y**, each with a different stroke dotted. Have the children write or trace the **Y** as you say the stroke description.

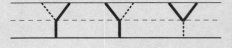

Families may use the stroke descriptions on the student page to encourage good letter formation at home. Copy and distribute **Practice Master 105** for children to take home for more practice.

Write the words.

yard   you   yell   yes

Write the sentence.

You can play with me.

 On Your Own Tell what games you like to play.

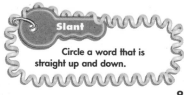
Slant
Circle a word that is straight up and down.

95

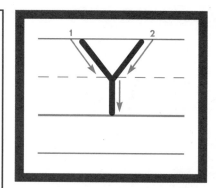

Touch the headline; **slant right** to the midline. Lift. Move to the right and touch the headline; **slant left** to the midline. **Pull down straight** to the baseline.

Fun and Games

 auditory   visual   kinesthetic

Letters by the Yard

Group the children and have them watch as you measure a yard of paper from a roll. Ask them to work cooperatively to fill the yard of paper with a yard of writing. Let them decide whether to write letters, words, or sentences and how to divide the task. Remind them to write carefully.

Yes/No Game Prepare two index cards with guidelines for each child. Have children write *yes* on one card and *no* on the other. Use the cards to play a listening game. Ask children to hold up a card to indicate their answer to fact or opinion statements such as these:

- **L** comes after **M** in the alphabet.
- I like to read.
- Yaks are large animals.

Apply

Before the children write the words and sentence on the page, write on guidelines on chart paper or on the chalkboard: *What is your favorite toy?* Include several letters with obvious errors in slant. Ask the children to help you identify the incorrectly written letters and to explain how they are wrong. Observe the children as they complete the page and respond to **On Your Own**.

Slant

Help the children evaluate the vertical slant of the letters they wrote by comparing them with the models. Then have them respond to the direction in the Key feature at the bottom of the page.

PRACTICE MASTERS 65–66

Name:

Write the letter and the words.

y y y y y y y y y

your   yet   yellow   youth

year   yum   young   hay

Copyright © Zaner-Bloser, Inc.   Practice Master 65

Yes!   Yasmine is happy.

Practice Master 66   Copyright © Zaner-Bloser, Inc.

Coaching Hint

Evaluation Using guidelines on the chalkboard, write a line of lowercase and uppercase letters with several obvious errors. Have children take turns using colored chalk to correct the errors at the chalkboard. (visual)

T95

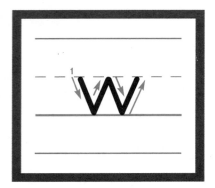

Touch the midline; **slant right** to the baseline. **Slant up** (right) to the midline. **Slant right** to the baseline. **Slant up** (right) to the midline.

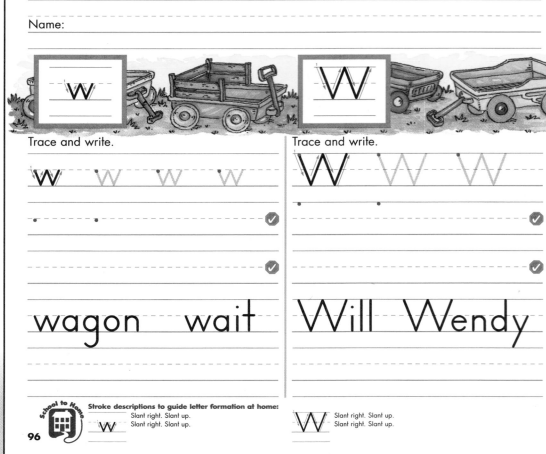

Name:

Trace and write.

wagon wait

Trace and write.

Will Wendy

Stroke descriptions to guide letter formation at home:
Slant right. Slant up.
Slant right. Slant up.

Slant right. Slant up.
Slant right. Slant up.

1. Present the Letter

Direct the children to look at lowercase **w**. Help them recognize that **w** is made of two **v**'s.

Model Write **w** on guidelines as you say the stroke description. Have the children use their finger to trace the model **w** in their books as you repeat the description.

Practice Let the children practice writing **w** on marker boards or slates or on other paper before they write on the pages.

2. Write and Evaluate

Ask the children to trace the shaded letters with pencil, beginning each one at the dot. Then ask them to write two rows of letters and the words with **w**.

✓ **Stop and Check** This icon directs the children to stop and circle their best letter.

To help them evaluate **w**, ask:
• Does your **w** have four good slant strokes?
• Is your **w** about the same width as the model?

*Repeat teaching steps 1 and 2 for uppercase **W**.*

To help children evaluate **W**, ask:
• Are the four slant strokes of your **W** straight and not curved?
• Is your **W** about the same width as the model?

Corrective Strategy

To help the children write **W** the correct width, place dots on the headline and baseline as shown. Point out that **W** and **w** differ in size but not in stroke formation. Stress the importance of using the guidelines.

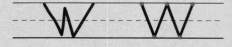

Families may use the stroke descriptions on the student page to encourage good letter formation at home. Copy and distribute **Practice Master 106** for children to take home for more practice.

T96

Write the words.

winter   wall   want   wish

Write the sentence.

Will it snow today?

On Your Own Tell what your weather is like today.

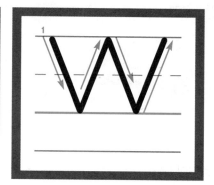

Touch the headline; **slant right** to the baseline. **Slant up** (right) to the headline. **Slant right** to the baseline. **Slant up** (right) to the headline.

Slant
Circle a letter that is straight up and down.

97

Fun and Games

auditory   visual   kinesthetic

Apply

Before the children write the words and sentence on the page, write the sentence on guidelines on the chalkboard, making several obvious errors in the slant of some of the letters. Read the sentence and ask if it is written correctly. Elicit that some of the letters slant wrong. Observe the children as they complete the page and respond to **On Your Own**.

Help the children evaluate the vertical slant of the letters they wrote by comparing them with the models. Then have them respond to the direction in the Key feature at the bottom of the page.

PRACTICE MASTERS 67–68

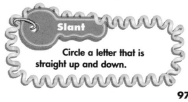

| Name: |
| Write the letter and the words. |
| w   w   w   w   w   w   w |
| white   wash   wet   work |
| wing   will   wood   wind |

Vve went to VVyoming.

Practice Master 68

Coaching Hint

Basic Strokes Using card stock or other heavy paper, cut out the parts of a letter (basic strokes) and have the children put the parts together to form the letter. (visual, kinesthetic)

Word Web Arrange string or yarn into a large web shape on a bulletin board. Add a paper or plastic spider. Distribute index cards with guidelines. After everyone agrees that *web* begins with **w**, ask children to write a word that begins with **w** on each card. Encourage the use of dictionaries and other books for ideas. Arrange the cards over the web to see the words the spider caught.

Action Word Charades Choose one player to act out an action word for classmates to guess. Remind children they are not allowed to give any oral clues, but explain that they can give one written clue by writing on the chalkboard the letter that begins the action word.

T97

Practice and Application

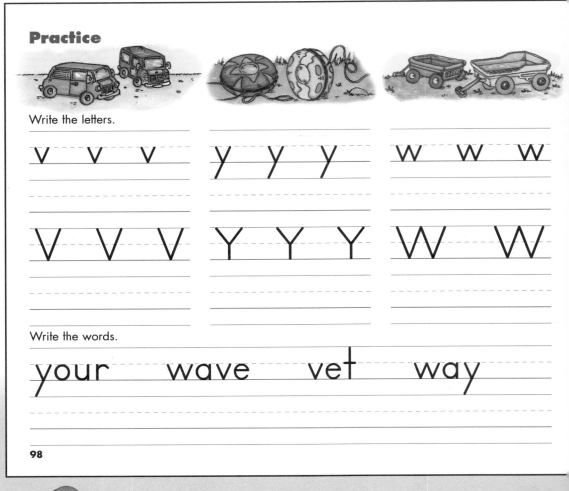

Practice

Write the letters.

v   v   v   y   y   y   w   w   w

V   V   V   Y   Y   Y   W   W

Write the words.

your   wave   vet   way

98

1. Review the Letters

Direct the children to look at the letters being reviewed on student page 98. Ask them what they remember about correct slant in manuscript writing. *(The writing is vertical.)*

Review the stroke descriptions and model again any of the letters the children may be having difficulty writing.

Ask a volunteer to give a verbal description of one of these letters: **v, y, w, V, Y, W**. Challenge the other children to identify the letter being described and then write it on guidelines on the chalkboard.

2. Write and Evaluate

Tell the children to write the letters, beginning each one at the proper starting point. Then have them write the words on the page. Remind children to refer to the models often and to make sure their writing is vertical.

✓ Stop and Check

To help children evaluate their lowercase letters, ask:
- Does your **v** touch the midline and baseline?
- Does your **y** touch the headline of the next writing space?
- Does your **w** have four slant strokes?

To help children evaluate their uppercase letters, ask:
- Do your **v** and **V** (and **w** and **W**) look alike except for size?
- Is the last stroke of your **Y** straight up and down?

Corrective Strategy

To help the children write **w**, remind them that all the strokes slant right.

W not W

More About Practice

Provide meaningful ways for beginning writers to use their new skills. Ask children to practice handwriting as they fill in class forms, make lists of favorite things, write cards and notes to classmates, and label pictures they draw.

T98

Application Write an invitation.

You're Invited!

When: Friday 4:00

Where: Valley School

What: a party

 Slant

Circle a word you wrote that has good slant.

99

Write Away

It's a Party! Invite the children to name holidays and special occasions they know. List them on the chalkboard. Have the children choose one and write an invitation to a party or get-together they want to host in honor of the day. Remind them to include When, Where, and What.

 Apply

Before children write the invitation on student page 99, ask volunteers to look at the page and describe what they notice about the slant of the writing. Remind them to write letters that are straight up and down. Observe children as they write on the page.

 **Slant**

Help children summarize what they have learned about slant. Then have them respond to the direction in the Key feature.

Special Helps

Drawing or writing on a vertical surface facilitates development and strengthening of the wrist and hand. When children color a picture on an easel or on the chalkboard at about face level, gravity helps to correctly position the wrist and hand for writing. The back end of the writing tool should be visible to the child as he or she works. As children become fatigued, check their writing position frequently.

—*Maureen King, O.T.R.*

Fun and Games

 auditory

 visual

 kinesthetic

Sense or Nonsense?
Write a story with fill-in blanks on the chalkboard. Ask the children to write in the blanks words or phrases that begin with **v, y, w, V, Y,** or **W**. Then enjoy the resulting story. Have volunteers read the story, a sentence at a time. Invite children to say whether each sentence makes sense or is nonsense.

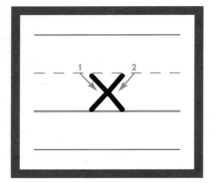

Touch the midline; **slant right** to the baseline. Lift. Move to the right and touch the midline; **slant left** to the baseline.

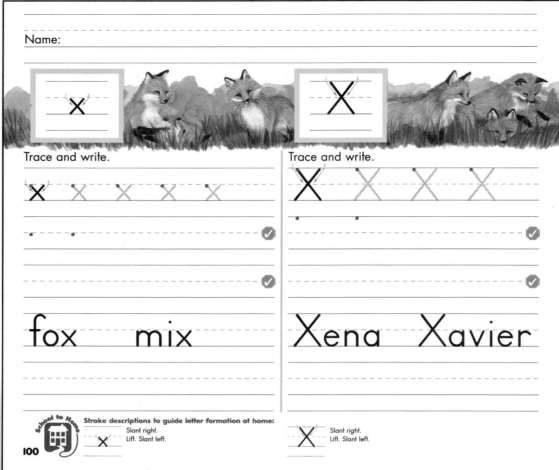

Name:

Trace and write.

X X X X X

fox   mix

Trace and write.

X X X X X

Xena Xavier

School to Home Stroke descriptions to guide letter formation at home:

100

X Slant right. Lift. Slant left.

X Slant right. Lift. Slant left.

---

1. Present the Letter

Have the children look at lower-case **x**. Focus attention on the letter's shape by helping the children recognize where the two slant lines in **x** cross.

Model Write x and X on guidelines as you say the stroke descriptions. Have the children compare the size and formation of the letters. Ask them to write **x** and **X** on their desktop with their finger as you say the descriptions together.

Practice Let the children practice writing **x** on marker boards or slates or on other paper before they write on the pages.

2. Write and Evaluate

Ask the children to trace the shaded letters with pencil, begin-ning ___ at the dot. Then ask ___ ite two rows of letters and the wo ds with **x**.

Stop and Check This icon directs children to stop and circle their best letter.

To help them evaluate **x,** ask:

• Are your slant strokes straight?
• Do your slant strokes cross halfway between the midline and the baseline?

Repeat teaching steps 1 and 2 for uppercase X.

To help children evaluate **X,** ask:

• Do your slant strokes cross at the midline?
• Is your **X** about the same width as the model?

Corrective Strategy

To help the children cross the slant strokes in **x** correctly, have them first make the slant right stroke. Place a dot on the midline where the slant left stroke should begin. Tell the children to aim the second slant stroke at the halfway point on the first slant stroke.

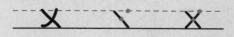

X X X

Families may use the stroke descriptions on the student page to encourage good letter formation at home. Copy and distribute **Practice Master 107** for students to take home for more practice.

T100

Write the words.

box   six   taxi   fix

Write the sentence.

X marks the spot.

 On Your Own Tell where you would hide a treasure.

Slant
Circle a word that is straight up and down.

101

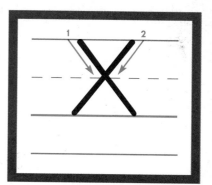

Touch the headline; **slant right** to the baseline. Lift. Move to the right and touch the headline; **slant left** to the baseline.

Fun and Games

 auditory   visual   kinesthetic

③ Apply

Before the children write the words and sentence on the page, call attention to the slant of the letters in all the words. Remind them to write carefully so their letters will have correct slant. Observe the children as they complete the page and respond to **On Your Own**.

 Slant

Help the children evaluate the vertical slant of the letters they wrote by comparing them with the models. Then have them respond to the direction in the Key feature at the bottom of the page.

PRACTICE MASTERS 69–70

Name:

Write the letter and the words.

X   X   X   X   X   X   X   X

next   six   wax   ox

ax   xylophone   exact

Copyright © Zaner-Bloser, Inc.   Practice Master 69

Xena is from Xenia.

Practice Master 70   Copyright © Zaner-Bloser, Inc.

Coaching Hint

Practice Too much practice of letters in isolation will discourage most children. Meaningful writing activities include friendly letters, jokes and riddles, nametags or labels, charts, vocabulary cards, and simple stories or poems. Writing may be done in cooperative groups.

Words With x Point out that **x** is a letter that does not begin many words but can be found in other positions in words. Write words that have **x,** such as *box, six, excellent,* and *Texas.* Choose volunteers to use their finger to trace each **x.** Provide dictionaries for children to use, and have them work in pairs to search for words with **x.** Ask them to list words they find.

Spaghetti Letters Invite children to use dry spaghetti to form the straight line and slant letters they have been learning. Demonstrate how to break the spaghetti and how to match the size of the pieces. Have children glue each spaghetti letter to an index card and then write the letter below it.

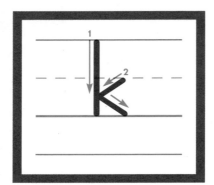

Touch the headline; **pull down straight** to the baseline. Lift. Move to the right and touch the midline; **slant left**. **Slant right** to the baseline.

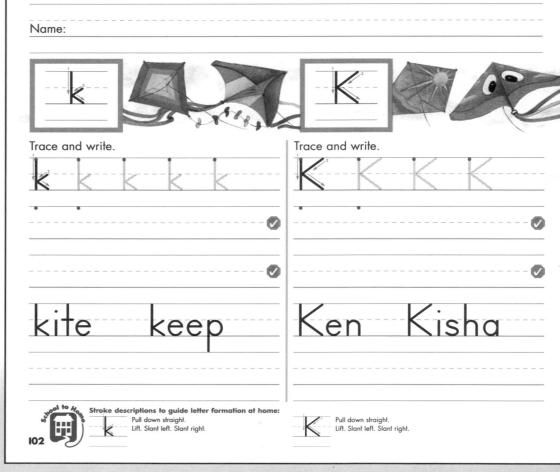

Name:

Trace and write.

k k k k k

kite   keep

Trace and write.

K K K K

Ken Kisha

Stroke descriptions to guide letter formation at home:

Pull down straight.
Lift. Slant left. Slant right.

Pull down straight.
Lift. Slant left. Slant right.

1. Present the Letter

Have the children look at lowercase **k**. Help them recognize that the two slant strokes touch the pull down straight stroke between the midline and the baseline.

Model Write **k** on guidelines as you say the stroke description. Invite the children to use their finger to trace the model **k** in their books as you repeat the description.

Practice Let the children practice writing **k** on marker boards or slates or on other paper before they write on the pages.

2. Write and Evaluate

Ask the children to trace the shaded letters with pencil, beginning each one at the dot. Then ask them to write two rows of letters and the words with **k**.

Stop and Check This icon directs the children to stop and circle their best letter.

To help them evaluate **k,** ask:

• Is your **k** straight up and down?
• Are your slant strokes straight and not curved?

*Repeat teaching steps 1 and 2 for uppercase **K**.*

To help children evaluate **K,** ask:

• Is your **K** straight up and down?
• Do your two slant strokes meet at the midline?

Corrective Strategy

To help the children correctly write the slant strokes in **K,** show how the slant left stroke stops on the midline where the slant right stroke begins. Place dots on the headline and the baseline to show the width of **K**.

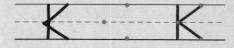

Families may use the stroke descriptions on the student page to encourage good letter formation at home. Copy and distribute **Practice Master 108** for children to take home for more practice.

TI02

Write the words.

kids   keys   kick   kiss

Write the sentence.

Kids like to fly kites.

On Your Own Tell what other things kids like to do.

Slant

Circle a letter that is straight up and down.

103

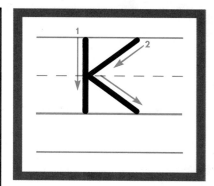

Touch the headline; **pull down straight** to the baseline. Lift. Move to the right and touch the headline; **slant left** to the midline. **Slant right** to the baseline.

Fun and Games

auditory   visual   kinesthetic

③ Apply

Before the children write the words and sentence on the page, emphasize that manuscript writing is straight up and down. Write *kick* correctly on guidelines on the chalkboard and then write it again with the letters slanting incorrectly. Discuss which model is correct and why. Observe the children as they complete the page and respond to **On Your Own**.

Slant

Help the children evaluate the slant of the letters they wrote by comparing them with the models. Then have them respond to the direction in the Key feature at the bottom of the page.

PRACTICE MASTERS 71–72

Name:

Write the letter and the words.

k   k   k   k   k   k   k   k

king   kit   know   knot

kind   knock   sock   talk

Copyright © Zaner-Bloser, Inc.   Practice Master 71

Karlo knows Kelly.

Practice Master 72   Copyright © Zaner-Bloser, Inc.

Coaching Hint

Shape Review uppercase letters with slant strokes. Write **M, N, W, V, X,** and **K** on the chalkboard. Have children choose two letters to compare. Ask: *How are they alike? How are they different? Which strokes are the same? Which letter has the most strokes?* (visual)

Spoonerisms Word pairs with switched first letters are called "spoonerisms." Write several word pairs such as these on guidelines on the chalkboard: *gold coat, big dog, yellow bell, bat call, tall man.* Guide children in switching the initial letters to create new word pairs. (For example, *gold coat* becomes *cold goat.*) Write the new word pairs on the chalkboard. Encourage children to write their own spoonerisms.

Phonics Connection
Write a list of words such as these on guidelines on the chalkboard: *black, rock, look, seek, like, take.* Read each word. Ask a volunteer to say a word that rhymes and write it on the chalkboard. Point out **k** in each word.

Touch the midline; **slide right**. **Slant left** to the baseline. **Slide right**.

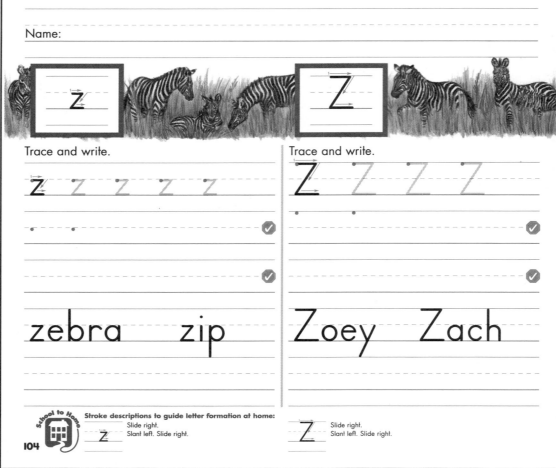

Name:

Trace and write.

z z z z z

zebra   zip

Trace and write.

Z Z Z Z

Zoey Zach

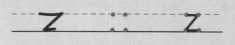
Stroke descriptions to guide letter formation at home:
z — Slide right. Slant left. Slide right.

Z — Slide right. Slant left. Slide right.

104

---

1. Present the Letter

Direct the children to look at lowercase **z**. Focus attention on the letter's shape by helping the children recognize the three straight strokes that make **z**.

Model Write **z** on guidelines as you say the stroke description. Model writing **z** in the air as you repeat the description. Have the children say the names of the strokes as they write **z** in the air with you.

Practice Let the children practice writing **z** on marker boards or slates or on other paper before they write on the pages.

2. Write and Evaluate

Ask the children to trace the shaded letters with pencil, beginning each one at the dot. Then ask them to write two rows of letters and the words with **z**.

Stop and Check This icon directs the children to stop and circle their best letter.

To help them evaluate **z**, ask:
• Does your **z** touch both the midline and the baseline?
• Are the top and bottom strokes of your **z** the same width?

*Repeat teaching steps 1 and 2 for uppercase **Z**.*

To help children evaluate **Z**, ask:
• Does your **Z** touch both the headline and the baseline?
• Are your lines straight?

Corrective Strategy

To help the children write **z** with straight lines, demonstrate how to pause before and after the slant left stroke. Remind the children not to lift their pencils and to make sure the two slide right lines are the same width.

z   z

Families may use the stroke descriptions on the student page to encourage good letter formation at home. Copy and distribute **Practice Master 109** for children to take home for more practice.

Write the words.

zoo   fuzzy   maze   zoom

Write the sentence.

Z is a zigzag letter.

On Your Own   Name things that zigzag.

Slant

Circle a word that is straight up and down.

105

Touch the headline; **slide right**. **Slant left** to the baseline. **Slide right**.

Fun and Games

auditory   visual   kinesthetic

Fonts and Sizes Have children work in small groups to examine magazines and newspapers to find examples of each letter in a variety of fonts. Display the letters, in alphabetical order, on a bulletin board or on mural paper. Discuss the shapes of the letters in different fonts. The letter **g,** for example, may have a simple curved descender: **g,** or a curly descender: **g**. Ask children to identify fonts that are more legible than others.

Alphabet Zoo Creatures Give each child a 5-inch oak tag square. Assign letters and have children use a marker to write their letters. Then have them use pencils and crayons to turn the letters into new zoo creatures. Have children label their creatures and arrange them in a zoo scene on a bulletin board.

Apply

Observe the children as they complete the page and respond to **On Your Own**. After they write, have them compare their letters with the models. Invite them to explain why correct slant is important in handwriting.

Slant

Help the children evaluate the vertical slant of the letters they wrote by comparing them with the models. Then have them respond to the direction in the Key feature at the bottom of the page.

PRACTICE MASTERS 73–74

Name:

Write the letter and the words.

Z Z Z Z Z Z Z Z Z

fizz   puzzle   prize   daze

maze   zipper   buzz   size

Copyright © Zaner-Bloser, Inc.   Practice Master 73

Zumar likes the City Zoo.

Practice Master 74   Copyright © Zaner-Bloser, Inc.

Coaching Hint

Practice Continue to emphasize the importance of good handwriting in all subject areas. Provide writing activities that encourage children's immediate application of handwriting skills.

Practice and Application

Practice

Write the letters.

x x x x   k k k k   z z z z

X X X   K K K   Z Z Z

Write the words.

buzz   zero   next   king

106

1. Review the Letters

Direct the children to look at the letters being reviewed on student page 106. Ask them to summarize what they remember about slant. *(Manuscript writing should be straight up and down; refer to the models for guidance when forming letters with slant strokes.)*

Review the stroke descriptions and model again any of the letters the children may be having difficulty writing.

Ask a volunteer to give a verbal description of one of these letters: **x, k, z, X, K, Z**. Challenge the other children to identify the letter being described and then write it on guidelines on the chalkboard.

2. Write and Evaluate

Tell the children to write the letters, beginning each one at the proper starting point. Then have them write the words on the page. Remind children to use correct slant.

✓ Stop and Check

To help children evaluate their lowercase letters, ask:
- Do your slant strokes in **x** cross about halfway between the midline and the baseline?
- Does your **k** have two slant strokes?
- Does your **z** have two slide right strokes?

To help children evaluate their uppercase letters, ask:
- Do your **x** and **X** (and **z** and **Z**) look alike except for size?
- Is your **K** about the same width as the model?

Corrective Strategy

To help the children write **Z**, remind them not to lift their pencils and to make sure the two slide right lines are about the same width.

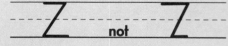

Z   not   Z

More About Practice

Spice up handwriting practice by asking children to write letters in a variety of ways: finger-trace on the back of their hand; dip their finger or a paintbrush into water and write large letters on the chalkboard; write letters in shaving cream on their desktop; write with large markers or crayons on chart paper.

T106

Application   Write the story of the Gingerbread Man.

Mix the batter.

Bake the cookie.

It zooms away.

My Words

Slant

Circle a word you wrote that has good slant.

Write Away

Storybook Photo Album Invite children to draw a picture of their favorite character from a storybook. Have them label their "photo" with a few words or a sentence. Put all the pictures into a large photo album and place it in the reading center.

3 Apply

Before children write the story sentences on student page 107, ask volunteers to look at the page and describe what they notice about the slant of the writing. Remind children to write with correct slant. Observe children as they write on the page.

My Words Ask children to write story words they remember from "The Gingerbread Man." Encourage them to write words that contain the review letters. If they need help, suggest they look for words on the previous pages.

Slant

Help children summarize what they have learned about slant. Then have them respond to the direction in the Key feature.

Special Helps

If a child has difficulty using the non-preferred hand to steady the paper when writing, try this activity. Prepare a lightweight cardboard stencil with three or four simple shapes cut out. Have the child anchor the stencil firmly against the chalkboard at about face height with the recessive hand (thumb up) while drawing in the shapes with the dominant hand. Lightly anchor the stencil with masking tape or poster-tac to assist children; but only as they begin this activity. In addition, using smaller pieces of paper, such as sentence strips, should help prompt the need to steady the paper.

—Maureen King, O.T.R.

Fun and Games

auditory   visual   kinesthetic

On-Stage Review with the children the story line in "The Gingerbread Man." Assign parts to volunteers, and invite them to act out the story for their classmates. Encourage other groups of children to act out other familiar and favorite stories.

Note: Some children may enjoy writing their own dialogue for the stories.

Before Writing

Write the following rhyme on chart paper and read it with the children, pointing to the words as you do.

> One, two, buckle my shoe.
> Three, four, shut the door.
> Five, six, pick up sticks.
> Seven, eight, lay them straight.
> Nine, ten—a big fat hen.

Have children identify number words in the verse. Then count to ten in Spanish, pausing after each number to have children repeat it. Write the words on the chalkboard. Have children match Spanish words to English words in the rhyme.

Invite children to share number rhymes they know in English, Spanish, and other languages.

Number Words Write the numerals and the number words.

1 one   uno   2 two   dos

3 three tres   4 four cuatro

5 five   cinco

On Your Own Write the Spanish words for **3** and **4**.

108

Review

Direct the children to look at the English and Spanish number words and the numerals on student pages 108 and 109. Ask them what they remember about the size of numerals. (*All are tall.*) Then ask what they remember about the shape of the letters in the words. (*All are made with one or more of the basic strokes in manuscript writing.*)

Review the stroke descriptions and model again any of the letters or numerals the children may be having difficulty writing. (Refer to pages T22–T25 for stroke descriptions and teaching strategies for numerals. See the table of contents to locate the teacher pages that introduce specific letters and their stroke descriptions.)

Write and Evaluate

Tell the children to write the numerals and the number words. Remind them to form their numerals and letters carefully so they will be legible.

To help children evaluate their numerals and number words, ask:

- Do all your numerals touch both the headline and the baseline?
- Are your numerals and letters written straight up and down?
- Are your horizontal strokes straight across?
- Are your circle strokes round?
- Does your writing have consistent vertical slant?

Write the numerals and the number words.

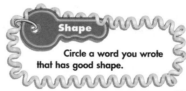

6 six   seis   7 seven   siete

8 eight ocho 9 nine nueve

10 ten diez

On Your Own Write a numeral and a number word to tell your age.

Shape
Circle a word you wrote that has good shape.

Write Away

Number Story Booklet Invite children to create a booklet with an illustration and sentence about each number word in this lesson. Encourage them to include number words in Spanish and English in their sentences. Remind them to write sentences neatly with correct spacing between letters and words. Have them point out a word or sentence that is neatly written on a peer's paper. Bind the pages and share the pictures and stories with others.

On Your Own

Ask children which words they are being asked to write on student page 108. Encourage them to write carefully and to compare their letters with the models to evaluate the legibility of their writing.

Have children respond to the writing prompt on student page 109. Encourage volunteers to tell which numeral they wrote. Then ask whether they wrote the number word in English, Spanish, or another language.

Coaching Hint

Evaluation Emphasize the importance of legible numeral formation whenever children write numerals. Discuss problems that can arise if numerals are not formed correctly. (visual, auditory)

Shape

Help children summarize what they have learned about shape. Ask them to choose several words they have written on the pages and evaluate their writing by comparing the shape of their letters with the models. Then have them respond to the direction in the Key feature.

Fun and Games

auditory   visual   kinesthetic

Our World, U.S.A. On a large piece of poster board or butcher paper, work with the children to create an imaginary map. Use names of the children in the class, such as Todd Town and the Rita River. Let the children make up distances between towns and other points on the map. Challenge the children to think of a name for the area shown on their map.

Before Writing

Write the chorus and first verse of "Here We Go 'Round the Mulberry Bush" on chart paper, underlining the day of the week. Prepare word cards, each printed with the name of a day of the week. Invite children to sing as you point to the words. Encourage children to make up new verses for each day of the week by adding phrases about things they do at school. Hold up the word card for the day as the children sing.

Chorus:
Here we go 'round
the mulberry bush,
the mulberry bush,
the mulberry bush.
Here we go 'round
the mulberry bush,
So early in the morning.

First Verse:
This is the way we
go to school,
go to school,
go to school,
This is the way we
go to school,
So early Monday morning.

Ask children what they notice about the first letter in the name of each day.

Days of the Week Write the name of each day.

Monday Tuesday

Wednesday Thursday

Friday Saturday Sunday

110

Write and Evaluate

Direct children to look closely at the letters in the words on student page 110 and to write the name of each day of the week under the model.

To help children evaluate their letters, ask:

- Do your tall letters touch both the headline and the baseline?
- Are your letters written straight up and down?
- Are your slant strokes pulled in the proper direction?
- Are your circle strokes round?

On Your Own

Point out to the children that a note is a very short letter. Identify the main parts of the note on student page 111 (*greeting, body, closing, signature*).

Ask children to think of a friend they might write a note to. Direct them to finish the note on the page.

Remind them to use the headlines and midlines in the writing space on the page to guide the size of their letters.

Encourage the children to write carefully and to compare their letters with the models to evaluate the legibility of their writing.

Write to a friend. Finish this note.

Dear _____,

Today is _____

_____

_____

_____

_____

Your friend, _____

_____

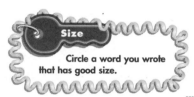

Size

Circle a word you wrote
that has good size.

III

Coaching Hint

Sitting Position Remind children to use correct body position when writing so they will write better. They also will not tire as quickly. Encourage them to sit comfortably erect with their feet flat on the floor and their hips touching the back of the chair. Both arms should rest on the desk. Be sure children are relaxed, holding their pencils correctly.

 **Size**

Help children summarize what they have learned about size. Ask them to choose several letters they have written and evaluate their writing by comparing the size of their letters with the models. Then have them respond to the direction in the Key feature.

You may want children to work with partners. Ask them to read their words to a partner and ask the partner to comment on the size of the letters in their note.

Write Away

Daily Diary Staple together seven pieces of writing paper. Invite children to keep a diary for one week. Explain that they will write about the things they enjoyed doing on each day. They might also include a note about the weather that day. To begin each page, have children write *Today is (day of the week)*. Provide time at the end of each day for children to read from their diaries.

Fun and Games

auditory	visual	kinesthetic

Design a T-Shirt Give the children a construction paper cutout of a T-shirt. Ask them to think about all the things they have enjoyed during the current school year. Encourage them to choose one thing and develop a design, a picture, or a brief message to decorate their shirt.

Before Writing

Write the following rhyme on chart paper, and underline *January*. Read it to the children. Then have them read it with you as you point to the words.

> Apples, peaches, pears, and plums,
> Tell me when your birthday comes.
> "January"—J-a-n-u-a-r-y

Repeat the verse, substituting each month, and have children stand when they hear their birthday month.

List the names of the months. Use tally marks to show how many children have birthdays in each month.

Months Write the name of each month.

January   February

March   April   May

June   July   August

112

Write and Evaluate

Direct the children to write the names of the months of the year on student pages 112 and 113, beginning each letter at the proper starting place. Remind children to space their letters carefully so they will be legible.

To help children evaluate the spacing in their writing, ask:
- Are your letters about the same width as the models?
- Do all your letters touch the baseline?
- Are any of your letters too close together?
- Are any of your letters too far apart?

On Your Own

Invite volunteers to tell which months with holidays they wrote and to describe how they used correct spacing when they wrote the names of those months.

September   October

November   December

On Your Own Write the name of two holiday months.

Spacing
Circle a word you
wrote that has good spacing.

113

Wall Calendar Cut 12 nine-inch squares of drawing paper and of writing paper. Divide the class into twelve groups and assign each a month. Invite each group to design two squares for a wall calendar: one with an illustration depicting something that usually happens in that month and the other with writing that describes it. Have children write the name of the month at the top of each paper, and arrange the squares to create a wall calendar. Have each group read aloud their sentences.

Coaching Hint

Spacing Make several sentence strips. Cut the words apart exactly where they begin and end. Place each cut-up sentence in a plastic or paper bag. Invite children, individually or in pairs, to arrange the words into sentences. Have them place their index finger or a craft stick between words to determine correct spacing. Then invite children to write the sentence with correct spacing on the chalkboard. (visual, kinesthetic)

Spacing

Help children summarize what they have learned about spacing. Then have them respond to the direction in the Key feature.

Fun and Games

auditory   visual   kinesthetic

Name and Frame It!
Make monogrammed frames using alphabet macaroni letters, white glue, and craft sticks. Demonstrate how to make a frame by gluing wooden craft sticks together to form a square or rectangle.

Have children complete their frames and label them with their names spelled in alphabet macaroni letters. Frames may be painted with thinned tempera paint. When the frames are finished, help the children use them to frame a good handwriting sample or a self-portrait.

The Importance of Speed in Handwriting

The goal of handwriting instruction is to enable children to write legibly with ease and fluency. It is important, however, not to stress fluency (speed) too early. Children should master writing the lowercase and uppercase alphabets before there is a concern for speed. At the first-grade level, we do not recommend emphasizing speed until the second semester. By the end of first grade, children should be able to write legibly, without stress, approximately 20 letters per minute. Based on this estimate, the children should be able to write the rhyme on student page 114, legibly and without stress, in about two minutes.

Why Write Quickly?

Discuss with the children times when being able to write quickly might be helpful or necessary. These might include writing a note in class, copying an address or telephone number from TV, jotting down ideas as they come to mind, writing words for a spelling test, and writing a story. Emphasize the importance of maintaining legibility even when writing quickly. Describe a time when you or someone you know wrote important information quickly—and were unable to read it later.

Coaching Hint

Automaticity The ability to write letters and words automatically allows children to spend more time thinking about the content of their writing. To make sure children are gaining automaticity, ask them to demonstrate correct letter formation with their eyes closed.

Writing Quickly

Make your writing easy to read.
Write this rhyme.

Rain, rain, go away.
Come again another day.

Now write it again.
Try to write faster.

114

Write and Evaluate

Direct the children to look at the rhyme on student page 114 and to read it with you. Review any letters that still present difficulties for any of the children. When the children seem comfortable with the task, have them write the rhyme the first time, trying to write a little more quickly than usual but still writing letters that are easy to read.

Note: If you want to make this an actual timed writing, have the children begin at your signal. After exactly one minute, have the children stop and put a mark, such as a star or a checkmark, after the letter they just completed. Then have them finish the rhyme.

Count the letters in each child's marked passage. Most first-graders can be expected to write about twenty letters legibly in one minute.

After the children write the rhyme, encourage them to evaluate their letters and words by comparing them to the models. Ask questions such as these:

- Do your letters have good shape?
- Do your tall letters touch the headline?
- Do your short letters touch the midline?
- Do **g** and **y** go below the baseline and touch the next headline?
- Do your words have good letter spacing?
- Is there good spacing between your words?
- Is your writing vertical?

Write the rhyme one more time.
Try to write faster.
Make sure your writing is easy to read.

Now read your writing. Ask others to read it, too.
Then circle Yes or No next to each sentence.

My writing is easy for me to read.   Yes   No

My writing is easy for others to read.   Yes   No

Writing More Quickly

Point out to the children the two writing grids at the bottom of student page 114. Explain that this space is where they are to write the rhyme again, trying to write faster than they did the first time.

You might wish to time this writing as you did the first time, signaling the children when to begin and when to pause after one minute and make a special mark.

Again, encourage the children to evaluate their writing, comparing it to the models and to the letters in their first attempt. Did they continue to write letters and words with correct shape, size, spacing, and slant?

Direct the children to look at the writing space on page 115 in their books. Point out that this space is where they are to write the rainy day rhyme one more time. Have

them try to write faster than they did during the other two times, but caution them not to sacrifice legibility at the price of speed.

For timed writing, follow the procedure recommended earlier in this lesson. Help the children evaluate their writing by comparing it to the models and to their previous attempts. Then have them respond to the evaluation checklist on student page 115.

Note: It is suggested that you have the children write the rhyme twice in one handwriting lesson and a third time during the next handwriting lesson. This should prevent the children from tiring and enable them to continue to write well and not feel stressed.

Evaluation

Self-evaluation is an important step in the handwriting process. By identifying their own handwriting strengths and weaknesses, children become independent learners. The steps in their self-evaluation process are as follows:

Question

Children should ask themselves questions such as these: "Is my slant correct?" "Do my letters rest on the baseline?"

Compare

Children should compare their handwriting to correct models.

Evaluate

Children should determine strengths and weaknesses in their handwriting based on the Keys to Legibility.

Diagnose

Children should diagnose the cause of any difficulties. Possible causes include incorrect paper or pencil position, inconsistent pressure on the pencil, and incorrect strokes.

Improve

Self-evaluation should include a means of improvement through additional instruction and continued practice.

Show What You Can Do

I can write lowercase letters from **a** to **z**.

I can write uppercase letters from **A** to **Z**.

116

Show What You Can Do

Invite children to share their thoughts about what they have accomplished in handwriting. Help them discuss their progress in writing letters with correct shape, size, spacing, and slant.

Explain that they will show what they can do on student page 116 by using their best writing to form the lowercase and uppercase letters. You may wish to allow children to use the writing implement they feel most comfortable with.

Practice

Let children practice writing letters on laminated writing cards or slates or on other paper before they write on student page 116.

Evaluate

To help children evaluate their writing, ask questions such as these:

- Are all your letters vertical?
- Are your letters with circles round?
- Do letters that go below the baseline touch the headline below?
- Did you dot your **i** and **j** and cross your **t**?
- Do all your uppercase letters touch the headline and baseline?

Note: Certificates of Progress (*Practice Master 77*) *should be awarded to those children who show notable handwriting progress and* Certificates of Excellence (*Practice Master 78*) *to those who progress to the top levels of handwriting proficiency.*

Finish the story.

Once when I was little, I went to

_____

_____

_____

_____

_____

_____

_____

_____

_____

_____

_____

Keys to Legibility
My writing has good shape. ☐
My writing has good size. ☐
My writing has good spacing. ☐
My writing has good slant. ☐

117

On and On Stories
Have children work in small groups to write a story. Suggest they decide on a topic and choose one group member to start the story by writing a sentence. Then ask members to take turns continuing the story by saying a sentence and writing it. Encourage them to share their completed stories.

Finish the Story

Before children write, encourage a lively sharing of ideas about the different subjects they might choose for their personal story. If you use a writing process in your class, have children follow it to complete the page. Allow them to use other paper for their composing before they write their completed story on student page 117.

Remind children to begin each sentence with an uppercase letter and to include an end mark. Accept the use of invented spellings.

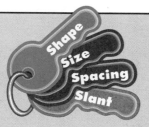

The Keys to Legibility

Remind children that the Keys to Legibility are helping them achieve their goal of legible handwriting.

Shape Four simple strokes—vertical, horizontal, circle, and slant—make it easy to write letters with consistent and proper shape.

Size Consistently sized letters are easy to read—and easy to write. Use the midlines and headlines to guide the size of the letters.

Spacing Correct spacing between letters in a word and between words in a sentence makes handwriting easy to read.

Slant Children have learned how to position their papers and hold their pencils so writing vertical letters comes with ease.

Fun and Games

 auditory visual kinesthetic

Rhyming Word Cards

Have children illustrate pairs of rhyming words on separate cards. Direct them to draw a picture on one side of the card and to write the word for the picture on the other side. Repeat for the second card. Children will discover the rhyming words by naming the pictures or by reading the words in each pair.

Handwriting and the Writing Process

If you use a writing process in your class, have children follow it to complete the writing activity on student page 118. The writing process steps might include the following.

Prewriting

What should I write?
During prewriting, children plan for their writing by making notes, lists, and webs. Carelessly written prewriting work may cause confusion throughout the writing process, but easy-to-read notes and webs smooth the way for students, teachers, and writing partners.

Drafting

I write my ideas in sentences.
Children's best handwriting isn't necessary for a first draft. In fact, concentrating on handwriting may take children's attention away from the content of their writing. However, a "sloppy" draft makes revising and editing more difficult. As children develop a consciousness about legibility, their writing will be fluent **and** easy to read.

Revising

What should I change?
As children revise their drafts, remind them to begin each sentence with an uppercase letter and to use an end mark. The drafting stage is also a good time to check

---

Handwriting and the Writing Process

Write about an animal you would like to see.
Write on a piece of writing paper. Follow these five steps as you write.

I. Prewriting
Plan ideas for your writing.
Use good handwriting so you can read your ideas later.

2. Drafting
Write your ideas in sentences.
Your writing should be easy to read.

3. Revising
Revise your writing.
Make changes so that your writing says what you mean.

4. Editing
Check your spelling, punctuation, and handwriting.
Make sure your writing is easy to read.

5. Publishing
Share your writing with others.
Use your best handwriting.

118

---

slant and spacing in the writing. As they revise, children should continue to be aware of the need for legibility.

Editing

How can I improve my handwriting and spelling?
To complete the writing process, have the children edit their drafts, checking spelling, punctuation, and handwriting. Thinking about legibility should always be part of the editing stage of the writing process. The **Keys to Legibility**—shape, size, spacing, slant—help children know what to look for.

Publishing

How will I share my work?
When publishing writing, it's especially important for children

to use their best handwriting. Neat, legible writing shows courtesy to readers. It makes a good first impression, and it helps ensure that readers will understand the writer's message.

Note: Legible handwriting is important during every stage of the writing process.

Record of Student's Handwriting Skills
Manuscript

	Needs Improvement	Shows Mastery		Needs Improvement	Shows Mastery
Uses good sitting position	☐	☐	Writes **e** and **E**	☐	☐
Positions paper correctly	☐	☐	Writes **f** and **F**	☐	☐
Holds pencil correctly	☐	☐	Writes **g** and **G**	☐	☐
Writes vertical lines	☐	☐	Writes **j** and **J**	☐	☐
Writes horizontal lines	☐	☐	Writes **q** and **Q**	☐	☐
Writes backward circle lines	☐	☐	Writes **u** and **U**	☐	☐
Writes forward circle lines	☐	☐	Writes **s** and **S**	☐	☐
Writes slant lines	☐	☐	Writes **b** and **B**	☐	☐
Writes numerals **1–5**	☐	☐	Writes **p** and **P**	☐	☐
Writes numerals **6–10**	☐	☐	Writes **r** and **R**	☐	☐
Writes **l** and **L**	☐	☐	Writes **n** and **N**	☐	☐
Writes **i** and **I**	☐	☐	Writes **m** and **M**	☐	☐
Writes **t** and **T**	☐	☐	Writes **h** and **H**	☐	☐
Writes **o** and **O**	☐	☐	Writes **v** and **V**	☐	☐
Writes **a** and **A**	☐	☐	Writes **y** and **Y**	☐	☐
Writes **d** and **D**	☐	☐	Writes **w** and **W**	☐	☐
Writes a question mark	☐	☐	Writes **x** and **X**	☐	☐
Writes an exclamation point	☐	☐	Writes **k** and **K**	☐	☐
Writes **c** and **C**	☐	☐	Writes **z** and **Z**	☐	☐

119

Record or Student's Handwriting Skills

The **Record of Student's Handwriting Skills** serves to indicate each child's progress in mastering the skills presented. The chart lists the essential skills in the program. After the skills that are listed have been practiced and evaluated, you will be able to mark the **Record of Student's Handwriting Skills** for either *Shows Mastery* or *Needs Improvement*.

Zaner-Bloser's *Evaluation Guide* for grade 1 handwriting is a handy tool for evaluating students' writing. The evaluation criteria are the Keys to Legibility. Samples of children's handwriting, ranging in quality from excellent to poor, provide a helpful comparison for evaluation.

Needs Improvement

If a child has not mastered a skill, provide additional basic instruction and practice. First, determine the child's specific needs. Then return to the initial teaching steps of the lesson for ways to help the child. To improve letterforms, have the child practice writing the letter in isolation and within words and sentences. Reinforce instruction through activities geared to the child's modality strengths. Ask the child to evaluate his or her writing with you. Reevaluate the child's writing following practice over time. When mastery of the skill is achieved, check *Shows Mastery*.

Note: *The* **Record of Student's Handwriting Skills** *is reproduced on* **Practice Master 76.**

Shows Mastery

Mastery of written letterforms is achieved when the child writes the letters using correct basic strokes. Compare the child's written letterforms with the letter models shown in the book. Keep in mind the Keys to Legibility (shape, size, spacing, slant) when evaluating letters, numerals, punctuation marks, words, and sentences for mastery of skill. Observation will indicate whether a child has mastered such skills as pencil and paper positions.

Check the appropriate box for each skill.

Index

120

Teacher Notes

Teacher Notes

Teacher Notes

Teacher Notes

Teacher Notes

Teacher Notes

Teacher Notes

Teacher Notes

I like to write le
friends. I alw
manuscript wri

I like to write le
friends. I always
manuscript w

I liKe to write
friends. I alway
manuscript writ

rage

etters to my

ays use my best

ting.

ir

etters to my

s use my best

riting.

or

letters to my

s use my best

ing.

3

ISBN 0-7367-1500-2

90000>

9 780736 715003